The Turnpik
Sunnisi
Marley Hill
Byermoor

by
F.G. Newman with Sunniside & District
Local History Society

Local people in pantomime at the Hobson Chapel.

Previous Page: Violet, May, Cecilia, Lily and Annie Douglas of Lingey Fine.

First published in 1998 by

The People's History
Suite 1
Byron House
Seaham Grange Business Park
Seaham
Co. Durham
SR7 0PW

ISBN 1 902527 01 1

Contents

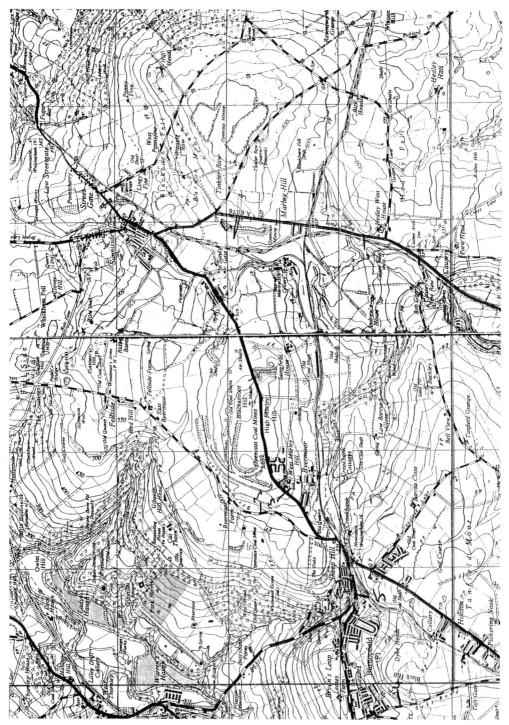

A map of Watergate to the Hobson.

Introduction

The Coming Of The Turnpike

Nearly 200 years ago, about 386 members of the 'Gentry' living in County Durham and Southern parts of Northumberland, decided to form a Turnpike Trust. Together they raised enough money to improve, repair and widen the road, from Lobley Hill to Burtree Ford, in upper Weardale, a distance of about 30 miles, and passing through Sunniside, Crookgate, Maiden Law, Lanchester and Wolsingham. In 1793, an Act was passed in Parliament, giving them the authority to carry this out. (The Act, included a Turnpike Road, from Crookgate to Black Hedley, via Burnopfield, Medomsley and Shotley Bridge, also, a road from Wolsingham to Durham City, via Crook and Brancepeth.)

Some of the local gentry involved with this Turnpike Trust were: Sir Thomas Clavering of Greencroft and Axwell Park, Sir Thomas Henry Liddell of Ravensworth, the Right Hon John, Earl of Strathmore, Anthony Leaton of the Whaggs, John Marley of Dunston, Ralph Carr of Dunston Hill, Jasper Harrison and Robert Hopper Williamson, of Whickham. In 1814, the Act of 1793, was renewed for a further 21 years. The number of Trustees were increased by 135, among the new subscribers were, Morton John Eden of Beamish, William Greenwell of Kibblesworth, George Thomas Leaton of the Whaggs and Richard Dobson of Gibside. The Trustees met once a year, to hear the surveyor's and treasurer's reports. At first they met at Wolsingham, but later, at the King's Head at Lanchester.

The work involved on the 4 mile stretch from Lobley Hill to Crookgate was considerable. The surveyor had the authority to open out quarries, to provide the necessary materials to make and widen the road. Quarries, which may have been used in connection with the road, were at Baker's Quarry in Washingwell Wood at Fugar Field, near the Tea Well at the Whinnies, where Fell View now stands at The Crescent. Along the way milestones were set in the ground, showing the distance between Wolsingham and Newcastle, they were placed beside the road at Green's Farm, at Low Streetgate; Sunniside Wood, opposite Fell View; at High Marley Hill and Crookgate. Guide Posts were erected at road junctions. The 1858, Ordnance Survey Map, marks one at Lobley Hill, another at Pennyfine Road, and one at Crookgate.

From the North Lodge (demolished in 1970) to Watergate, involved building retaining walls to support the bankside and building a small bridge over the Black Burn. There was a boundary stone at Blackburn Bridge, separating Whickham and Lamesley Parishes. At Watergate Bank, just below the lodge, a culvert was made beneath the road to accommodate the millrace, known as the Trench, which wound its way for one and a half miles, from the Black Burn in Washingwell Wood to the Corn Mill at Cow Close. At Fugar, a bridge was built over the wagonway early in 1841. The bridge was partly rebuilt in 1908, to allow the higher 20 ton coal trucks to pass beneath it. In 1967, five years after the last set of trucks went down the incline, the steel bridge with stone buttresses was removed and the road re-aligned, at a cost of £15,000. Up till then, road users had to negotiate a narrow sharp 'S' bend over the bridge.

At Low Streetgate, the road was straightened and raised. The Marquis of Granby Inn, though rebuilt, still stands at the original road level, the old house was built in 1783. An earth retaining wall was also built, opposite the pub. The road winds through the old hamlet of Streetgate. Prior to 1794, the road from Streetgate went up the Fell, to Tinkler Row, then along to the Causey, down to Beamish Burn, up to Stanley and on to Maiden Law. The Turnpike Road abandoned this route and a new road was made, up to High Marley Hill, Crookgate, Flint Hill, Catchgate, re-joining the old route at Maiden Law. Between The Crescent and Marley Hill, the workmen making the road dug a cutting through a hillock, composed of sand, then made an embankment at the bottom of Church Bank. There used to be a boundary stone here, beside the road,

Looking east to west up the Old Road.

separating Whickham and Lamesley Parishes, but it was made obsolete when Marley Hill Parish was formed.

The Trustees had the power to collect tolls. Tollgates were placed at Fugar, (still referred to as Fugar Bar, by many people, long after the bar was removed), at Crookgate and further on at Catchgate and Maiden Law. The gatehouse at Crookgate was called the Crook and was wedged in the fork of the road, near the bottom of Crookbank, so that it could collect tolls from both the Wolsingham and Shotley Bridge roads. (This toll-house was demolished about 1910.) A ticket was issued to the traveller, allowing him to pass through the bar. On the ticket was the date, amount of toll paid and the type of conveyance. Pedestrians paid nothing, they passed through a smaller gate or over a ladder stile. People evading payment or those assaulting the gatekeeper, could be fined from between £2 - £5 by the local Magistrate. Toll charges could be changed but 21 days written notice had to be given and displayed at Turnpike Gates, main road junctions and in the Newcastle newspapers.

In fixing the tolls, the Trustees were mindful of the amount of damage done to the road surface, and those vehicles which dug deepest into the road paid the higher tolls. Wagons drawn by oxen, as compared to those drawn by horses, paid less tolls, for oxen were less likely to damage the road surface with their hooves. The toll charges paid on wagons were rather complicated, owing to the combination of factors to be taken into account - the number of wheels, the width of the wheel rim, and the number of horses or oxen pulling the wagon. Payment of tolls was exempt in certain cases, for example carriages, horses, etc. which passed along the Turnpike for less than 100 yards. (People using the road in between Fugar and Crookgate, out of sight of the Toll Houses did not pay anything.) Payment was made only if you passed through the toll-bar. The farmer had to pay tolls when he drove his livestock to market at Newcastle.

The Turnpike Road certainly helped to stimulate trade and was therefore a success, but having served their purpose the bars were removed from the road at Fugar and Crookgate, some time in the mid 1870s. Luke Fenwick and his wife Jane, were the last toll collectors at Fugar. Older folk can remember the tollhouse at Fugar standing until the early 1930s. Mrs Annie Stott moved there after retiring as landlady of the Middle House (1902).

Reference: Turnpike Acts of 1793 and 1814 (Lobley Hill to Burtreeford) from Newcastle City Library.

6

WATERGATE TO STREETGATE

Mining at Watergate.

The Colliery royalty stretched for two miles, from the Black Burn in Washingwell Woods to Mitcheson's Gill in the south, because of its width it also included Ravensworth Park and the castle. The top seams had been extensively worked in the seventeenth and eighteenth centuries. A wagonway was laid from Ravensworth Park Farm and through the woods to meet up with the Team Colliery Wagonway. In the 1600s Thomas Liddell had worked coal mines in the wood beside the Black Burn and in 1884 the Earl of Ravensworth along with Charles Perkins & Partners had sunk a shaft in the yard at the castle with a view to mining coal deposits. Priestman Collieries Ltd sunk Watergate Pit (pictured) in 1923, the Haswell shaft (upcast) was mainly for man-riding and the Garth shaft (downcast) was for bringing up coal. Ponies were used underground in the early years pulling tubs carrying 12 cwt of coal or stone. A lot of modern machinery was installed to increase productivity, but there were quite serious problems with excess water. In December 1953 a new underground railway was completed at a cost of £40,000. It was almost two miles long stretching from the shaft bottom right up to the coal face and it carried the men in and out. The seams worked in the Watergate area were the Hutton, Beaumont, Top Busty, Bottom Busty, Tilley and the Brockwell. The coal mine became less and less viable over the years and in August 1964 it closed.

Marshall Lands

The land lies to the north of Fugar near Streetgate beside the Blackburn and Washingwell, between Broom Lane and Fugar Bar. On 16th January 1609 permission was given to Lionel Maddison for the acquiring of Marshall Lands and the Paddocks in Whickham from one Richard Hinde. In the same year Lionel obtained a lease to work coal at Marshall Lands and the lease was renewed in 1624 for a further 15 years. By 1632 there had been thirteen pits sunk in the area near Fugar Field and there was also a stone quarry.

Toward the end of the eighteenth century George Rawling and his wife Margaret, daughter of Edward Liddell of Ravensworth, lived at Marshall Lands. Then George Maddison took over followed by Joseph Hall in the early 1800s who became tenant farmer of 113 acres. His son Tom ran the farm with his sister Mary as Housekeeper until 1897. John Johnson farmed Marshall Lands prior to the First World War, followed by John Barron until 1932. In 1917 Messrs Priestman's Collieries bought farmland in the Watergate area including 192 acres at Marshall Lands. Joseph Tate then took over the tenancy of the farm followed by his son Leslie in 1939 who also ran Washingwell Farm, his other son Noel eventually took over Old Sunniside Farm. Leslie was one of the first farmers in the area to possess a combined harvester. In 1987 William Oates of Ouston Spring Farms Ltd took over and bought the 250 acres centred around Marshall Lands.

Right: Bill Hudspith of Beech Street, Sunniside pictured here leading the horse worked at Streetgate Farm for many years. Up on the hay cart is Bobby Laybourne.

Streetgate Farm

William Thirlaway was the farmer in 1841, his sons John and Thomas continued until around 1860. James Swan (1820-89) came from Lingeyfield to take over the farm, his father James Swan snr farmed at Ravensworth Hillhead from 1830-40 and his brother Robert was the farmer at Old Ravensworth. Streetgate Farm covered 110 acres but seven acres were lost when Watergate Colliery was built. In the late 1940s the farm had fifteen dairy cows and Bobby Swan was one of the last local farmers to deliver milk on a horse drawn float. The farm employed local people and gave jobs to many children when potato picking. In 1991 the farmhouse was renovated and the outbuildings cleared to make way for housing development named Streetgate Park.

The Streetgate Murder

On Monday 28th August 1865 the annual flower show was held on the Ravensworth Estate and afterwards there was a dance held in a marquee adjoining the Marquis of Granby Inn. Whilst the dance was in full flow all was not harmony in the kitchen of the inn, much to the annoyance of the landlord, William (Bill of the Bank) Laidman. A group of drunks were engaged in a furious argument during which threats of violence were made. A wandering cobbler and notorious villain, Jack Bee took exception to a man called Joseph Leybourne siding with a young farm servant named Nixon. Overhearing the row, some of the men employed on the Ravensworth Estate joined in making things considerably worse. The discord continued until closing time, because of the flower show an extension of drinking hours had been granted to the inn.

A lady living next door to the inn was alarmed to hear a violent row taking place at two in the morning. She heard threats being yelled at Joseph Leybourne by a voice she could not identify as they wandered off up the hill towards Sunniside. A short while later the dance was over and the inn closed, the noise had died down and people were wandering off home. A well known local man, George

The Marquis of Granby Inn where the violent row began.

Mudd and some companions had not gone far up the hill, when they spotted a man sitting on a stone and propped up by a hedge, he appeared to be sleeping. One of the men carried a lantern and shone it into the face of the 'sleeping' man. The group were shocked to see a very dead Joseph Leybourne with gaping wounds in his head and blood covering his face. The men used a makeshift stretcher and carried the body to his home which was almost opposite the Rose Shamrock & Thistle Inn. At an Inquest held on Friday 22nd September 1865 a verdict of 'wilful murder' was returned against 'person or persons unknown'. The local policeman, Miles (Miley) Robinson assisted by other officers looked for evidence with a view to bringing the murderer to justice. Several people were interviewed, among those one or two were suspected, including some individuals from the Ravensworth Estate. George Mudd was a man of such good character that he was never considered as the perpetrator. The most likely culprit was Jack Bee the travelling cobbler who died not long after the murder. He had met the other men present on the night of the row in the Marquis, probably to get their story right. Opinion was divided, some felt that Bee was capable of the murder although he strongly denied it, others stated that although a ruffian, Bee was not a murderer. There are differing reports on whether or not Bee stood trial, one report stated that he stood trial but was acquitted for lack of evidence. One thing is absolutely certain, we will never know the truth about who killed poor Joseph Leybourne.

Lingey Fine Gardens and the Douglas' Who Have Lived There
Written by Colin Douglas

The great upsurge of industrial development on Tyneside in the nineteenth century, attracting thousands of immigrant workers and their families to work in the steelworks, shipyards, engineering works, coal mines and coke works, brought with it the need, not only to house them but also for a change in the basic food supply chain. The rows of back to back terraced houses made no provision for feeding the families from the kitchen garden, which was a normal feature of the semi-rural areas such as Gateshead prior to this time.

The need for market gardens to provide a supply of seasonal vegetables to the new urban areas was a consequence of the population growth and many more were established. They tended to be located in fertile areas within reasonable transport distances from the greengrocers retailing them to the local population. Transport in those days was, of course, by horse and cart, except in those areas served by the railways, so that the Sunniside area, four or five miles from Gateshead, was an ideal location.

Lingey Fine Gardens on Pennyfine Road was owned by the Ravensworth Estate and had already been such a market garden for more than fifty years when William and Mary Douglas with their six children moved there from Gateshead in 1905. There were three boys, Bill, Stanley and Alfred and three girls, Cecilia, Annie and Elizabeth. Sadly, Elizabeth did not enjoy a long life, she died in 1905. Shortly afterwards, the birth of triplet girls in the family attracted a great deal of interest. This was because in addition to being a rare event, the fact that all three babies survived the multiple birth was far from

The original Douglas family of Lingey Fine, *circa* 1905. Back row, left to right: William (father), Bill, Mary (mother), Cecilia. Front row: Elizabeth, Stanley, Alfred, Annie.

usual in those days. The girls were named May, Lily and Violet, three flowers, as befitting the daughters of a market gardener. The family was completed in 1907 with the birth of another son, Frederick.

The pattern of the market garden business barely changed over the next forty years or so, with seasonal vegetables grown and supplied directly to local consumers, hawkers and greengrocers in Gateshead. Cabbages, cauliflowers, sprouts, lettuce, peas and beans

Field workers weeding and thinning out lettuce for Douglas Brothers.

were the stock in trade. Tomatoes were grown in greenhouses in summer. Rhubarb, forced in heated sheds and blacked out heated areas in the greenhouses in winter and grown outside in spring/summer, was a speciality.

William purchased the property when much of the Ravensworth Estate was sold to pay death duties in the 1920s and during this period some of the children developed and moved on. After service in the Armed Forces during the First World War, Bill emigrated to Australia where he farmed in Northern Queensland and near Brisbane. His surviving family still live there. Cecilia married and moved on but later returned with her daughter Marion and lived at Lingey Fine until 1947. Marion emigrated to New Zealand and still lives there near Nelson. Cecilia joined her and spent many happy years there prior to her death. Annie and May both married and lived as close neighbours for many years in Gateshead where May is still living. Lily married Bob Craig and lived on Sunniside Road for the rest of her life. Violet continued to live at Lingey Fine until 1947 when she married and spent the rest of her life in Sunniside with her husband Norman Curry. Stanley and Alfred also married, living at Pennyfine Road and Streetgate respectively, although Alfred spent some time in New Zealand late in life before returning to live near Durham. Frederick, or Teddy, as he was generally known, started work at Lingey Fine after leaving school at fourteen years of age and following the death of his father in 1941, he took over the business and moved into the house.

Towards the end of the Second World War a partnership was formed bringing the market garden businesses which Stanley owned on Pennyfine Road and Alfred owned at Streetgate together with the Lingey Fine enterprise to operate under the title of 'Douglas Bros' based at Lingey Fine. Alfred brought to the partnership a range of retail outlets as well as great expertise in plant and flower growing. Stanley had a well established customer base of wholesale firms located at the old Newcastle Green Market. The partnership acquired additional land, new greenhouses were erected and corn and potatoes were added to the range of crops.

Market gardening at that time was a highly labour intensive business, particularly during the summer. Large numbers of local people were employed in gangs very often out in the fields at dawn, harvesting cabbage, cauliflowers and lettuce, to be supplied fresh to the range of customers on that same day.

Frederick and his wife Sally, who had three children, Colin, William (Bill) and Freda, continued to live at Lingey Fine until 1971 when they retired and moved to Whickham. Frederick died in 1973 and Sally still lives in Whickham. Colin served in the Merchant Navy and reached the rank of Master before leaving the sea in 1961 to become H.M. Inspector of Factories.

He subsequently served as a Company Director of Swan Hunters, British Shipbuilders and other Companies before retiring from a position as Chairman of North Durham Acute Hospitals N.H.S. Trust in 1998. He and his wife Helen live in Whickham and have three sons, Stephen, Kevin and Andrew. Freda emigrated to America in 1964 and is now a Professor at the University of Southern Maine. She is married and lives with her husband John and their children Alexa and Jarad near Portland, Maine. Bill joined Douglas Brothers in 1960 after studying for a Diploma in Agriculture at Edinburgh University; sadly he was killed in a car accident near Andrews Houses in 1968. His wife Muriel now lives in Spain, their two sons Grant and Stuart live in France and Gateshead respectively.

The Douglas' of Lingey Fine Gardens		
Name	Born	Died
William	1865	1941
Mary (née Hedley)	1869	1945
Cecilia	1895	1982
Annie	1896	1988
William	1899	1976
Stanley	1900	1961
Elizabeth	1902	1905
Alfred	1903	1974
May	1906	
Lily	1906	1993
Violet	1906	1983
Frederick	1907	1973
Sarah (née Foster)	1908	
Colin	1933	
Bill	1939	1968
Freda	1942	
Stanley	1933	
Hazel (née Reed)	1933	1980
Stanley	1953	
Adam	1963	
Hazel (née Adamson)	1953	
Richard	1979	

Stanley's son, also named Stanley has worked for Douglas Brothers since leaving school and acquired the business following Frederick's retirement. He moved into the house with his wife Hazel and their two sons, Stanley and Adam. In 1976 he moved into a bungalow newly built on the Lingey Fine site, and his son Stanley with his wife, also called Hazel occupied the house; they have a son Richard. The two Stanleys, father and son continue to run the Douglas Brothers business.

The picture that emerges is one of nearly a century of very little change (1850-1950) in the pattern of market gardening, growing seasonal vegetables for local consumption with accelerating change over the past forty years or so. Mechanisation mainly in the form of tractors and their new specialist attachments have substantially reduced the need for the large numbers of workers who were required from time to time. Importers bringing in unlimited supplies of cheap vegetables from all over the world to the Team Valley Wholesalers and to supermarkets have significantly reduced the demand for locally grown produce.

New opportunities have been developed by Douglas Brothers, however, and Lingey Fine gardens now houses a well patronised garden centre selling a comprehensive range of garden plants and equipment as well as decorative fish and aquarium accessories. Happily there is also still a demand from discerning customers wishing to acquire the high quality, fresh seasonal vegetables which have been grown by the Douglas' of Lingey Fine for almost a century.

Lingey Fine Gardens, *circa* 1908 with Alfred Douglas.

The Douglas triplets – May, Lily and Violet, *circa* 1908.

Bill, Colin and Freda Douglas.

Douglas Brothers have given employment to many local people over the years, listed below are just some of those people:

Harold Atkinson, Nora Beck, Alice Boyd (née Burridge), Frances Boyd, Joyce Boyd, George Burns, Lesley Burns, Edith Brown, Irene Cant, Norma Cant, Raymond Carr, Ronnie Cloe, Peter Cloe, Alan Cloe, Paul Cloe, Brenda Collins, Kenneth Craig, Annie Croft, Roly Cunningham, Michael Dougan, Matthew Dougan, John Douglas, Philip Douglas, Joan Douglas, Mary Elliot, Evelyn Foster, Marjorie Graham, Les Harrison, Betty Hopper, Sadie Henry (née Chisholm), Violet Morrison, Lizzie Muncaster, Leiley Musgrove, Alice Newman (née Shorten), Sylvia Oddy, Maureen Ridler, Clare Ridler, George Rutherford, Manie Rutherford, Mrs Sanderson, Mrs Simpson, Irene Storey, Tom Turnbull, Mavis Vickery, Nellie Vickery, Freddie Vicarage, Minnie Vickery, Kathy Warner, Daphne Watson, Sheila Watson.

Left to right: Roger Potts, Alice Boyd, Annie Croft, Marjorie Graham.

Out in the Field. Back row, left to right: Annie Thirlwell, Violet Morrison, Joan Douglas, Brenda Collins, Minnie Vickery, Irene Snowball. Front row: Mary Elliot, Sadie Henry, Joyce Boyd, Jennie Douglas, Lizzie Snowball.

Left to right: Leiley Musgrove, Bryan Douglas, Norma Cant, Marjorie Graham, Freddie Vicarage, Alice Boyd, Mrs Wallace.

Lizzie Proudlock of Hillhead Farm seen here during a particularly bad winter being given a lift by Robbie Proudlock to Kibblesworth School where she was a teacher. Lizzie and Mrs Douglas were great friends.

Ravensworth Castle

To the east of Pennyfine Road lies Ravensworth Wood which contains the remains of the magnificent Ravensworth Castle. An early historian of County Durham explains the name:

'The antiquity of this castle leads to conjectures as to the etymology of the name; in many old records it is called Ravenshelm and Ravenfwaith, in the old spelling Raffenfweath. The Danish standard was called Raffen, and Weath is a north country word, now used in Scotland for sorrow. The assumption we would make is, that Ravensworth Castle is of Danish foundation, and had its name from them as Raffens-Helm, or the stronghold of the Danish standard; and that some defeat of that people had occasioned the name of Raffens-Weath, or Danish woe.'

The Danish warriors sailed up the north seas and visited this area, they anchored their fleet at the mouth of the Team. It is interesting to note that the Danes called natives of this

Lord and Lady Ravensworth on the occasion of their Golden Wedding celebrations, 9th October 1916.

Ravensworth Castle prior to its sad demise.

area 'Jordi's' meaning 'strange dark people', is this where our regional name 'Geordies' originated? Other words in common use among the Dane's were 'yem' which meant home and 'bairn' meaning 'boy child', we of course use the name to embrace all small children.

'When Denmark's Ravens o'er the seas

Their boding black wings spread,

And o'er Northumbrian lands and leas,

Their gloomy squadrons sped.'

Over the centuries the ownership of the castle changed hands. Around 1166, Bishop Ranulph Flambard granted Ravensworth and Hecton (now called Eighton) to his nephew Richard, a relative of the Barons Fitz-Marmaduke. On the death of the last in the male line of the Fitz-Marmadukes, Ravenshelm Castle then passed to the Lumleys when Eleanor Fitz-Marmaduke married into one of that ilk. In the time

A group of local lads on the Ravensworth Estate in the early 1900s.

of Bishop Hatfield, 1367, Alexander de Kybblesworth held the land. There followed many changes where names such as Gascoigne of Gawthorpe, Fitz-Hugh, Turneaux, Marmion, Dacre, and Parr appeared.

Under the date 1607 in the Registry Office at Durham, a record of acquisition by Thomas Liddell of the family estate at Ravensworth was held. It is the document by which Bishop James granted the manor of Ravenshelme and Lamesley from William Gascoigne, Knight, and Barbara his wife. This was the introduction of the family who would hold the Ravensworth estates for 300 years.

The castle was visited over the years by many noteworthy figures; the Duke of Wellington, Sir Walter Scott and Queen Victoria and Prince Albert to name but a few.

Reference: *Romantic Ravensworth* by Clarence R. Walton.

Ravensworth Hillhead Farm

The farm lies to the east, just off Pennyfine Road, between the Blackburn and High Park Woods. George Rawling was the farmer in 1802, his brother Tom was farming at Marshall Lands. Rawling was followed by James Swan (1786-1862) who farmed there in the 1830s and '40s. His brother Robert (1808-79) was farmer at Old Ravensworth. In the nineteenth century Hillhead covered almost 300 acres and the old house stood right on the boundary of the Fell. This was destroyed by fire in 1973 and a new house was built near the road. In front of the old farmhouse grew a small orchard sheltered by a high wall, beyond the garden stood an old farmworker's cottage. Initially the farm was supplied with spring water feeding from the Fell, but after opencast mining in the late 1940s this supply stopped and mains water was installed. Robert C. Proudlock (1825-1900) came to farm at Hillhead in 1876 from Hartburn, in 1886 he was the

Robert and Margery Proudlock with their children Robbie, Lizzie and Mary.

owner of a prize-winning Clydesdale stallion bred at Carlisle and named 'Ravensworth'. There was a lot of money to be made if one was fortunate enough to own a high calibre animal, accordingly the stallion was hired out for stud services. The charge was £2 (a considerable sum in those days) for each mare served, £1 to be paid first week in July and £1 when the mare proved to be in foal, with 2s 6d to be paid for groom's fee on first service. The Proudlock's son, also named Robert, eventually took over Hillhead Farm, he married Margery Shotton (the daughter of Edward and Mary Shotton of Old Sunniside Farm) and they had three children, Lizzie, Mary, and Robbie; there were three generations with the name Robert. The Proudlocks farmed at Hillhead for over ninety years. Lizzie taught at Kibblesworth School, she walked to and from Hillhead every day. Mary, Lizzie and Robbie never married. They sold the farm in 1970 and moved to Streetgate where they remained for the rest of their lives. From June 1970 to date, 1998, Harry Norman has farmed at Hillhead.

Mary and Lizzie outside of the Old Hillhead Farmhouse.

Loosing Hill Farm

In 1841 Mary Richardson farmed 149 acres and Amos Richardson was the farmer from 1846 until 1862. By then the farm had expanded to 175 acres, it employed four men and a boy. In April 1862 a sale of farm stock and implements of husbandry took place at the farm on behalf of the late Mrs Richardson. Over the years to come the farm changed hands on a number of occasions, Will Brabban in 1868, Cuthbert Carr in 1871, John Thompson in 1879, Matthew Watson in 1890, John Rutherford in 1894, Michael Dobson in 1910, Will Smith in 1914 and Robert Harcus in 1925.

When Durham County Council bought the farm from the Ravensworth Estate they divided it into two tenancies. In 1910 John Jobling took over the tenancy of one half of the farm and by the late 1920s he had taken over the entire farm staying there until 1945. The farm became commonly known as 'Joblings'. It was mixed arable, in 1925 they had 22 cows and Harry Wallace delivered their milk around the houses. Mr Jobling leased a field behind the farm to Sunniside Rangers AFC with players changing their clothes in the back room of the Travellers Rest Inn at Sunniside. The Sunniside Carnival was held at the farm in the 1920s and 1930s, there was a fairground atmosphere with stalls set up in the field and a jazz band playing. The Sunday school children from the nearby Chapel often had their summer tea outing at the farm and the children of the White Elephant School, across the road from the farm, used to visit the animals.

The Jobling family eventually moved to a farm in Yorkshire. The next tenant at the farm was Thomas Crisp who was followed in 1965 by John T. Robson. By 1990 the farm was unoccupied and Durham County Council planned to convert the farm buildings into homes. They also planned to build houses to the east of the old farm. In 1994 the County Council sold 45 acres of land to the Woodland Trust and it has been turned into a wildlife haven with trees planted and a walkway for the public.

The farming Rutherford family. Left to right: Sep Rutherford, Tom Rutherford, Bella Nicholls (née Rutherford), Lizzie Rutherford, Anthony Rutherford, Charlotte (Lottie) Brabban (née Rutherford) and Matthew Rutherford.

The White Elephant School at Streetgate

A school class in the early 1950s with teacher Jean Dawson. The school teaching staff over the years were: Hannah Armstrong 1923-48, Lesley Cuthbert 1923-51, Ethel Smith 1923 (pupil teacher), Elizabeth Morgan 1941-42, Ethel Sample 1941-46, Jean Lamb 1946-49, Mrs Binks 1949, Jean Dawson 1949-55, Mabel Davison 1951-62, Clare Doran 1955-62, Mrs A. Grant 1963 to closure in 1963. Edward Dodsworth (Caretaker) 1923-29, Charlotte (Lottie) Brabban (Caretaker) 1930-44, Jane Elliott (Milk/Meals) 1943-58, Louise Weightman (Dining Centre) 1946-54, Gladys Bell (Dining Centre) 1946-54, Jean Shepherd 1958-63, Mr Thompson (Boilerman) 1958-63, Freda Harrison 1961-63, Mrs Legg 1961-63, Mrs Cree (Road Crossing Patrol).

A school class, *circa* 1956, with head teacher Mabel Davison (1951-62) on the left and Clare Doran (1955-62) on the right.

SUNNISIDE

It's always stood on top of a hill
I think, if I'm right, it stands there still
Its name is known by far and wide
A little village called Sunniside.
If you want to get there by the easiest way
Get a bus that runs on the Kings Highway.
It's good for your health, you'll enjoy the ride
And soon you'll land at Sunniside
Two pubs there stand at the corner end
With names that invite you to come and spend
An hour or so with kindly folk
Who will bid you welcome with homely pride
These canny folk of Sunniside.
Just across the road you'll find the Chapel
Where good folk meet to pray and sing
Led by the choir under Uncle Bill
The Angels stop to listen in - to Sunniside.
There is no Chemist shop or cinema
No Doctor or Dentist your nerves to jar
We've a Post Office, a Co-op, a Blacksmiths shop
And a chap called Dick Clark to see you off
If you like a game of football in our village you'll find
A famous football team which leaves the rest behind
All budding internationalists, this with modest pride
They are known as the Imperials and live at Sunniside
Early in the morning when day has just begun
You'll find a little lady at the rising of the sun
Tramping down the roadway and door to door she calls
Opens up the letter box, and as the letters fall
You'll gently whisper to yourself
There's Mercy for us all - at Sunniside
We've had some grand old men, some of the best -
Will Fenwick, Tom Young, Jack Craig, now gone to their rest
Some remain with us, still in fine fettle -
Jack Wallace, Joe Harrison, Sep Rutherford, Matt Heppell
Grand chaps to meet and others beside
When you pay us a visit to old Sunniside
It's a grand place to live in, green fields all around
To Sunniside folk it is all hallowed ground
It's the next place to Heaven so the good record states
For just round the corner you'll find Peters Gates - at Sunniside.

By Sidney Easton of Hole Lane, *circa* 1948.

Sunniside Cobblers Shop

One of the most successful and certainly one of the longest reigning small businesses in Sunniside was Boyd's Cobblers Shop. Robert Swann Boyd worked at Whickham Colliery and at the age of 21 he unfortunately suffered a spinal injury. He was taken to hospital by horse and cart and the injury was so severe that the Coal Miners' Union man, with undue haste, went to see Robert's wife, to ask if she wanted the Colliery Band to play at his funeral. He did of course recover and was so determined not to sit around, that he worked for a time as a 'knocker up' to miners who lived in the Teams and Redheugh area. Robert and his wife Frances had six sons, Ernie, Jimmy, Billy, Bobby, George and Ralph who died in infancy. They also had four daughters, Jenny, Annie, Frances and Alice who sadly also died in infancy. He was taught how to repair footwear and started his own cobbling business in his back yard. He eventually opened a little shop on Askew Road, Gateshead, where he was helped by his 12-year-old son Ernie. Robert handed that shop over to his son, Jimmy when he decided to move with his family to nearby Sunniside. They moved to 5 Prospect Terrace, Sunniside Road, in 1932. Jimmy later moved to Sunniside. Robert bought some wood following the demolition of the old Army huts at Scotswood, Newcastle, then with the help of a friend, on the front gardens of Prospect Terrace, he built a hut. Although no bigger than 8 ft x 10 ft it was to be a family business that would stand for many years. Robert and his helpers moved the hut in sections to the site he had selected opposite the Methodist Chapel on Sun Street. Robert Swann Boyd spent 50 years as a cobbler. Regardless of the fee Robert repaired everything with a craftsman's care. He would advise heel or toe plates for the lads' boots, to make them last longer, or he would give a handful of hob nails or sprigs, so that fathers could

Jimmy Boyd (right) with bicycle, Tom Strong standing and Dave Armstrong up on the cart collecting footwear for repair, at Elm Street, *circa* 1935.

Frances Jane and Robert Swann Boyd.

carry out repairs themselves. He retired in 1961 leaving his son Ernie to carry on the business. Robert died aged 78 years.

Ernie Boyd, born in 1920, was to carry on the business until his retirement. He spent 56 years as a cobbler while his brother, Jimmy spent more than 30 years in the business. Ernie remembers as a small boy going around the houses to collect footwear for repair. During the Second World War, when leather became rationed and did not provide enough work, Ernie joined his brother Jimmy down the Pit. That was the only period of time he spent away from the cobbler's bench apart from wartime service. During his working life the Annual Rates of the shop rose from seven shillings and tenpence in 1932 to one hundred and fifty pounds in 1986. The price of leather had also risen dramatically, to five pounds per pound in weight.

Over the years Ernie carried out repairs for generations of some families. His craftsmanship was acknowledged by some famous figures; among his customers were Lord Gort from Hamsterley Hall, and the man who was to become the most famous of all Newcastle United footballers, Hughie Gallagher, also brought his shoes to Ernie for repair. Ernie remembers other customers of note, Dr Miller, and especially the Byermoor Priest, Father Austin Pickering. The land surrounding the cobblers was developed for the Barden Park Luxury Housing Complex. They could not demolish the Cobblers Shop without Ernie's permission. Ernie retired in November 1986 and owned the shop until 1993, when he allowed a Stanley Company to demolish it to create more space for an adjoining garden. The shop had been a landmark of Sunniside for 61 years. That home-made shed had provided a valuable service for the local people. It had also provided a modest living for Robert Swann Boyd and his son until they both retired. Ernie reflects that life was much happier in those days with a smaller community; even though most people were relatively poor, crime and violence in the village was almost unheard of. There is no doubt that Ernie valued his trade because it brought him into close contact with people and because of that he felt that he had enjoyed a happy working life.

Robert at the door of his shop at Askew Road, Gateshead prior to his move to Sunniside in 1932.

Some of the children of Robert and Frances, from left to right: Bob, Jenny, Jimmy, Annie, George, Ernie and Frances.

Ernie Boyd with his mother Frances, his wife Joyce and his father Robert.

Ernie Boyd The Cobbler

If you take the road up Lobley Hill and turn left at the top
As you're approaching Sunniside you'll find a little shop,
It's not at all imposing in fact it's very small,
It's only because I live there that I know it's there at all,
The shop is owned by Ernie an unpretentious kindly man,
Where he goes to make a living in the best way that he can,
You'll find him at his work bench where he works from early morn,
He's repairing other people's shoes, those that they've outworn
To ev'ry customer who calls he'll give a friendly willing smile,
Or else he'll stop and chat to them for just a little while,
He will talk about the local news and chat about the weather,
Or tell you what he thinks about the shocking price of leather,
This pleasant man of simple heart in life has one ambition,
It is to come and meet you Frank, perhaps there in your Mission,*
In this, though I don't agree with him, I'll honour his point of view,
I'd prefer he got the accolade as The Master of the Shoe.

* Radio Personality Frank Woppat

Written by Barbara Kinnarny

Ernie Boyd prior to retirement in November 1986.

The east end of Front Street, Sunniside, *circa* 1910. The front of Granby Terrace can be seen to the right of the photograph. Robert Thirlaway (1759-1831) took possession of three acres of land between Sunhill and Alexandra Terrace. His son William began to build Granby Terrace on that land in 1841, beginning at the top near the old Chapel. By 1856, William's son owned the terrace. The family were quite affluent, running the Granby Arms at Low Streetgate and running Streetgate Farm. To the left lies Sun Street (built in 1911) with the Methodist Chapel and the Sun Inn visible at the bottom.

The Travellers Rest Inn. Originally the Greyhound Inn built on the site around 1858, the first tenant was Robert Fenwick who was also a cobbler. In the 1870s he was followed by Alex Livingstone who also worked at Marley Hill coke ovens. By 1891, the pub was renamed The Board and was run by George Stott who was once a butcher at Streetgate, his brother William (Billy) was tenant at the Rose Shamrock & Thistle. The Greyhound was renamed the Travellers Rest by 1894. Pictured in the doorway is publican Richard Dillon (1863-1948) who was the tenant in 1910. Around 1912 the stone house was replaced by larger premises, which still stands today.

Directly opposite what was once the Travellers Rest is the Sun Inn run by William Wilson in 1841. By 1850, William Rutherford was Licensee although the pub was run by his wife Elizabeth whilst he supplemented their income by working at Marley Hill Colliery. He was followed by William Surtees in 1856 and in 1861 Robert Storey was the Licensee, although his wife Dorothy ran the pub with the aid of her daughters while he too worked at Marley Hill Colliery to help out financially. In those days most right minded people could not afford to visit the pub for every session and drink heavily so there was not a lot of money taken across the bar, hence the need for some Landlords to work elsewhere. The Storey family originated from Wylam and lived for a time at Marley Hill Hole (The Valley) in the early 1850s. In 1866 the Sunniside Benefit Society was formed and held their meetings at the Sun Inn. The membership was restricted

Margaret Davison (née Brabban).

to women only and operated much the same as a savings club. It was also a type of insurance, paying out funeral benefit from their funds. In 1873 Robert and Reuben Storey held the licence and by 1879 James Davison was in charge of what was now named the Rising Sun. James had married a widow, Mrs Margaret Brabban (pictured) the daughter of Robert Storey. James died in 1888 but Margaret continued to run the pub helped by her son William Brabban until her death in 1907.

The pub then passed to Joseph Davison, (pictured with his family in the back yard of the pub). Joseph died in 1915 at the early age of 39 years and his wife Louisa continued to run the pub. Jimmy Davison (standing next to his mother) became the Landlord in 1934. With his wife Ivy (née Johnson) they ran the pub until their retirement in 1955. Their only son, Stuart (who was married to Joan Strong) chose to follow an

Joseph and Louisa Davison with their children.

electrical career and did not take over the tenancy. Arthur and Doris Scorer left the Marquis of Granby to take over the Rising Sun following the retirement of Jimmy Davison. After the death of Arthur, in 1978, once again a widow became licensee and Doris ran the pub admirably until her retirement in 1983.

The west end of Sunniside, *circa* 1920. Dewhurst Terrace was built around 1902 and provided the major shopping facilities in the village. Over the years names very familiar to the local people have came and gone; Mrs McAvoy had a drapery shop at No. 18 in the early 1950s, this was replaced by an 'off licence' until 1993. Police Constable R. Shillaw lived at No. 14 in the 1920s, Ethel Mason ran a newsagent shop at No. 16 and eventually married Ben Irwin, who owned a cobblers shop at the Chapel Opening across the road. In the early part of the 1920s, Jim Shorten opened a fish & chip shop at No. 13 Dewhurst Terrace, he originally lived at Alexandra Terrace but eventually moved to The Crescent with his wife Anne. In 1956, Jim and Lillian Dunphy took over the fish shop and retired in 1983. Around 1928, Larry Dunphy ran a fish & chip shop in a wooden hut at the bottom of the Store Bank, Old Sunniside. Harry Ord had a chemists shop at No. 12, he was followed by Wm and Sydney Blackburn. The shop eventually became a newsagents in 1952 when Tommy White bought the premises. The shop at No. 9 was ran as an off licence and general dealers and changed hands a number of times, the Greys, Blackmores, Lucas', Fishers, Gelstones and Hopkins' passed through. The last person to run the shop as a general dealers was Alma Kelly (née Newman). She eventually sold the shop to Ralph Crowder a chemist who owns the business to date, 1998. The Sunniside Branch of Burnopfield Co-op was opened in July 1911 and ceased trading in 1987. Following various changes the building burned down on Thursday 12th March 1992. The Co-op store employed many people over the years and listed below are just some of the staff who worked at the Co-op from the 1930s until closure:

Managers: Mr Stonehouse (Co-op), Joe Croft (Butchers), John O'Neill (Grocery), Tom Ellison (Grocery), Bill Cruddace (Drapery), Bill Gibson (Grocery), J. Fawcett (Grocery), J. Davison (Drapery), E. Bradley (Grocery), Betty Morton (Grocery) and Betty Heron Manageress until the closure of the Store, Mr Hewetson (Chemist).

Delivery: Fred Armstrong (Van), Jack Burridge (Orders), Bill Lowdon (Milk), A. Burton (Van).

Staff: D. Fenwick, Betty Heron, R. Beck, A. Wilson, R. Cook, T. Ellison, A. Bell, C. Sanderson, Betty Morton, Mary McConnon, Alison Young, M. McKie, L. Gibson, Heather Wallace, Alie Newman (Chemist's Assistant until its closure).

Sunniside Folk

Edna and Rebecca Armstrong, Grove Terrace, Peters Gates, *circa* 1917.

Left to right: Dick Lowdon, Tom Liddle, David Armstrong (married Nancy English of Fugar Bar, 31st May 1941), George Armstrong, *circa* 1933.

The Alfreds family. Sammy (played the double bass in Marley Hill Colliery Band) with his son Billy, seen here holding Billy jnr and Mr Alfreds snr.

Best known as 'Reeds Butcher' and immensely popular, Jack Johnson (born 1st October 1901, died 4th August 1980) with his wife Esther (née Randle – born 19th December 1905, died 12th June 1989). Pictured here on 7th February 1970 at Marley Hill Miners' Welfare Hall.

In the days before television, video recorders, computer games and many more modern day leisure pursuits, people looked on a trip to the cinema (pictures) as a treat. Probably the highlight of the year would be the annual trip to the seaside. Streets would organise between them, book a bus and give themselves a well earned day out. Sunniside Club also gave members families an annual trip to the seaside, there used to be a fleet of buses lined up outside the Club. The men would go dressed in their best, sit on the sands without removing their jackets, no matter how hot, then dead on the dot of 11.00 am, 'opening time', they would make a beeline for the nearest Workingmen's Club and stay there until 'closing time', returning in high spirits. Pictured here from Sunniside are back row, left to right: Elsie Laybourne and Mrs Alfreds. Front row: first lady unknown, Mrs Hudspith and Eva Gibson.

Because we are so close to Newcastle the vast majority of people support Newcastle United AFC (the Black & Whites). In the past our team has achieved much. In 1969 they won the Fairs Cup by beating Ujpest Dozsa of Hungary. United won 3-0 at home and 3-2 away. The team was McFaul in goal, full backs Craig & Clark, left half Moncur (captain), right half Gibb, centre half Burton, centre forward Davies, outside left Foggon, inside left Arentoft, outside right Scott and inside right Robson. This was of course before current positions such as 'sweepers' and 'strikers'. Pictured here, proudly holding the trophy, are left to right, local men: John Storey, Jack Hudson, Bill Brown, Norman Storey.

Mary Jane Blackmore lived at Hazel Cottage and in 1962 was Sunniside's oldest resident reaching the grand old age of 101 years. Mrs Blackmore was born on 20th July 1861 near Tavistock and came north when she was only three years old. Her father lost his life in an explosion at Seaham Colliery. She married John Blackmore, a coal miner at Marley Hill Colliery, they had six children, four sons and two daughters. Unfortunately John died at the age of 68 years. She was a regular Chapel goer and read her bible every day. On her 100th birthday she received a telegram from the Queen. Sadly Mary Jane Blackmore passed away in 1963 just before her 102nd birthday. At the time of her death her family had expanded to eight grandchildren, twelve great-grandchildren and three great-great-grandchildren.

Mercy Mitcheson, September 1932. Mercy is mentioned in our introductory monologue which refers to her job as Postwoman for Sunniside and occasionally for Marley Hill too. She lived at No. 8 Alexandra Terrace and is pictured here in her garden. A very popular person who knew everyone in the village, she never failed to deliver mail regardless of dreadful weather. It is easy to picture her struggling through mountainous snow drifts carrying her huge mail bag and still finding time to have a cheery word with her many friends. Mercy never married and died in March 1962.

Bill Shorten, February 1945. Richard William (Bill) Shorten was born in 1898. He lived at Prospect Terrace in his younger days and was a coal miner at Marley Hill pit for most of his working life. He served in the Royal Artillery during the First World War and even though exempt from service he volunteered to serve in the Second World War but was too old. He joined the Home Guard and eventually became Officer Commanding. On the 1st January 1942 he received a commendation from the Lieutenant General Chief of Staff for services rendered. He had led a team of fellow miners and tunnelled into the wreckage of the bombed buildings on Fernville Avenue to save trapped residents and recover bodies. A popular figure, he played the

trombone in the Colliery band and sang at concerts as well as giving an occasional song at Sunniside Club. Bill married twice and had two children James and Elizabeth (Betty). He died in 1982 at the age of 84 years.

The local branch of the Agricultural Workers' Union. Bill Hudspith of Beech Street, Sunniside is kneeling, second row from the front and second from the right. The branch used to meet in the back room of the Travellers Rest Inn.

John Cadwallender of Sun Street with his sister Miriam, *circa* 1910.

Reeds The Butchers
Written By Colin Douglas

The premises at Gateshead Road, Sunniside, alongside the United Methodist Chapel comprising of butchers shop, slaughter house, stables, laying up shed and house were newly built by Edward (Ned) Reed in 1919 when he returned after service in the First World War. He established a partnership with his younger brother John (Jack) who had also served during the war. For the next forty years or so the firm of E. & J.R. Reed was the premier butcher in the area, providing meat, poultry and cooked produce. They supplied from both the horse and cart and later provided a door to door service by motor vehicle. The two brothers were members of a remarkable family of ten, five boys and five girls (pictured right). Edward snr originated from Haydon Bridge, Northumberland where he had worked as a stonemason. He came to Marley Hill Colliery where his skills were in high demand. A man of many parts, he eventually became winding man at the colliery and lived with his wife and family at Colliery Houses. For his retirement

The Reed family at Marley Hill in 1903. Back row, left to right: Bob, Maggie, Edward, Annie, Bill. Front row: George, Bella, Edward, Hannah, Alice, Cissie, Jack.

he had Haydon House built at Streetgate, this name served as a reminder of his origins. His son, Ned, who had served an apprenticeship as a butcher at Burnopfield Co-operative Society, set up in business as a butcher on his own account in premises behind the newly built house. Jack was the youngest son of the family, and after leaving school and prior to his war service worked part time for Ned in the butchery business. He also worked for another brother, Bob, who had a painting and decorating business in Sunniside. Ned's son, Bill, became a partner following his father's death in 1947. Jack's son, Michael, joined the business on leaving school in 1946 and after his National Service in the R.A.F. he ran 'The Pork Shop' in Stanley. Jack moved into Harperly Hall, Tantobie in 1948 and following the sale of E. & J.R. Reed in 1968, Bill moved on to a farm in Northumberland. Michael founded a garage business with Peter Gavin and today runs the Gavin Reed business in Sunniside. The original butchery premises are currently vacant, perhaps a casualty of progress succumbing to the growth of the supermarkets. Many local people will have fond memories of Reeds the Butchers, a traditional village shop with friendly banter between staff and customers, all behind us now but recalled with immense pleasure.

Reeds The Butchers

Edward (Ned) 1888-1947. John Rutherford (Jack) 1893-1977. William (Bill) 1921-1990. Michael 1930-.

The shop and house newly built, *circa* 1919. Left to right: Sid Clark, Ned Reed, Maggie (Ned's daughter), Jenny (Ned's wife) and Jack Johnson.

Jack Reed with his favourite horse and cart delivering meat at Dolly Town, Byermoor, *circa* 1926. Members of the Reed family were involved in many other local business ventures, with Maggie establishing the general dealers shop close to the butchers, trading as Maggie's and later as Middleton's.

Perhaps the most noticeable achievement was that of the five brothers, Bob, Bill, George, Ned and Jack, who in the early 1920s set up a bus company based at newly built garage premises on the corner of Beech Street and Sunniside Road, which are still in multi occupancy providing vehicle services. At the onset this was a part time 'venture' which operated under that title with each of the participating brothers continuing in their respective jobs. The Venture Bus Company expanded to become one of the major bus operators in North West Durham. Ned, Bill and Bob became full time directors of the company, which was taken over in 1970 by the Northern General Bus Company.

Old Sunniside Farm

The only surviving building of what was once known as Old Sunniside is the farmhouse, everything else, the surrounding houses and the farm buildings, are gone. The siting of the farm was part of what was once known as Gellesriding. Predictably the land changed hands over the years and just as predictably those famous names of bygone years appear, Clavering, Blakiston, Brignall, Liddell, Harding, Marley and Grainge.

In 1645 the Blakiston family owned Gellesfield, it eventually passed on to the Brignall family. The property of Thomas Brignall passed on to his wife Florence and grandchildren following his death around 1685. His grandson, Brignall Grainge, eventually inheriting the property until his death in 1701. His son, Henry Grainge who married Anne Middleton of Seaton, held the property until his death in 1781, his son Middleton Grainge then became the new owner. In what was once a dairy within the old farmhouse is a table tomb to the memory of Cuthbert Grainge who died in 1731. Middleton Grainge was the last of the landed gentry to live at Old Sunniside Farm, following his death in 1845, the farm was rented to tenant farmers. The estate covered 98 acres and received a further 31 acres from Blackburn Fell and a 5 acre plot from Whickham Fell.

The Shotton family ran the farm until around 1892. Robert Shotton sometimes drove his cattle from Sunniside to Satley, his relatives Anthony and George Shotton farmed there. Robert's nephew, Tom Head assisted him on the farm in the 1860s, Tom married the housekeeper Mary Ann Dobson. By 1890, the tenants were Edward and Mary Shotton with their eight children. Then the Routledge family took over from the Shottons around 1892 and farmed there until 1940.

On 13th May 1940 Reuben Noel Tate (born Christmas Day 1912) took over the farm, his father Joseph farmed Marshall lands. Noel increased food production and his contribution to the Second World War 'Dig for Victory' effort was significant. In 1941 he married Jessie Reed of Whickham Lodge, they had two children, Joseph, born 20th March 1944, and Kathleen, born 8th July 1946.

The farmhouse is quite imposing, the front was rebuilt with brick in the middle of the eighteenth century. There is a bricked-up window on the first floor which was probably done to achieve exemption from the old 'window tax'. The rear and side walls are part of the original stonebuilding, the front has four bays and may once have had an attic storey. At the front of the house was a small room with an upward curving ceiling, known as the 'prayer cupboard'. There was once

Tom Strong with his nephew, Thomas Gaul delivering milk from Routledges to Elm Street in the 1930s.

a pond to the west of the farm but one of Noel's predecessors had it filled in. Directly in front of the house was the farm gate with large stone pillars, this separated the farm from the houses.

Noel commenced farming with three, then four Clydesdale horses. They gave way gradually after Noel bought his first tractor in 1944, although a horse drawn reaper/binder made in early 1908 remained in use until 1947. During the war wheat was the main crop and three of the

Noel Tate at the rear of the Old Farm.

pasture fields were ploughed up to facilitate this need. After the war the farm consisted of one third pasture and two thirds arable. During the 1940s, Noel contracted steam threshing teams, it took a day to thresh ten to twelve tons of corn. He grew fields of potatoes and turnips and gave employment to hundreds of local men, women and children over the years. In bygone days children were expected to go potato picking during the school holidays to help supplement the family income. At one time there were short horn cows at the farm and Noel started a door to door milk delivery service. He also kept sheep but experienced terrible problems through local dogs 'sheep worrying'.

During the Second World War, on the night of 12th May 1941, a German bomber dropped his bombs on Sunniside, possibly in error or because he wanted rid of them to make his way home. One landed on the houses at the bottom of Fernville Avenue, one on the houses at the top of the street and one in the farm field directly between the lower lane and top lane (known as Bowmans Lane). The bombs had landed in a straight line at approximately 100 yard intervals, which was fortunate for the farmhouse standing less than 100 yards adjacent to the line of bombs.

Noel farmed at Sunniside until October 1988. After some 49 years he retired. It is probable that he found it a wrench to leave, but after so many years of following an arduous profession he had earned his retirement. The farm had gone, developers had cleared the way for the building of the Old Farm Court estate and had bought the farmhouse from him. He and Mrs Tate moved to Beadnell on the east coast, their daughter Kathleen also lives there. Kathleen and her husband own Sea Life Museum at Seahouses. Joe, his wife Pauline and family live at South West Farm, near the bottom of Whickham bank.

Jessie Tate with children Kathleen and Joseph.

An aerial view of Old Sunniside Farm and the surrounding area. Note how Kingsway ended at the farm gates and the gravel lane continued on to sweep across the fields and on to Fellside Road. Fernville Avenue, at that time the north extreme of Sunniside, can be seen in the background. All that remains today is the farmhouse.

Noel Tate at work during the harvest with Sid Easton, who had the farm at the bottom of Hole Lane. The farmers would assist each other when necessary. Shelley's Wood at the bottom of Metal Bank can be seen in the background.

Joe Tate and Eddie Nichol assisting on the same day. Joe's father and Sid Easton can be seen on the tractor in the background.

The Coronation of Queen Elizabeth II, 1953.

To celebrate the Coronation of the Queen, people organised street parties; saving for months to ensure a day of festivity with plenty to eat, drink and to provide souvenirs for the children. Unfortunately, on Coronation day the heavens opened making street parties impossible. Thanks to the

community spirit of those days the children were not to be disappointed. Noel Tate gave the use of his brand new barn to the people of the Council Houses and Matty Lowdon gave the use of his garage to the people of Beech Street and the surrounding area. The local people above are pictured in Matty's garage. Sitting on the right of the middle row is Mrs Margaret Hudspith with daughter Anne on her knee, her husband Bill with sons Robert, John and Tony are in the front row on the ground.

Pictured in Noel Tate's barn, standing from right to left: Bob Hickson, Mrs Hickson, Annie Shorten, Billy Murray, Jenny Gaul, Bobby Gaul, Bill Shorten, Sam Treglown, Sammy Alfred, 'Hanker' Gibson, Mrs Treglown, Pa Bridges. Seated, left to right: Sarah Vickery, Tommy Bland, Mrs Cant, Nancy Armstrong, Mrs Murray, Mrs Alfred, Ma Bridges. Seated on the ground, on the left, is Nelly Vickery and on the right, Maisey Cant.

Robert (Bob) Lowdon (born 7th May 1909 - died 1982) married Lilian Chambers Duncan pictured below. At the time of their wedding he was a fruiterer, delivering door to door. He also served in the Army during the Second World War. Bob and Lilian lived at Old Sunniside then at 27 Kingsway, Sunniside. He is pictured here with his horse and cart in the 1930s.

Lilian Chambers Duncan (1910-77), of 18 Elm Street, married Robert Lowdon, of 3 Elm Street, at Marley Hill Church on 7th December 1929.

Right: Lilian Lowdon (née Duncan) by now residing at Old Sunniside, pictured here with son Robert (Bob).

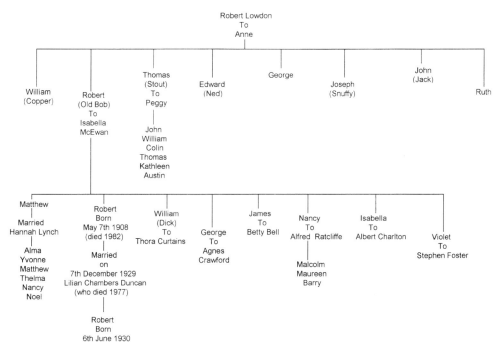

LOWDON FAMILY TREE

Robert Lowdon
To
Anne

William (Copper) | Robert (Old Bob) To Isabella McEwan | Thomas (Stout) To Peggy | Edward (Ned) | George | Joseph (Snuffy) | John (Jack) | Ruth

John
William
Colin
Thomas
Kathleen
Austin

Matthew

Married Hannah Lynch

Alma
Yvonne
Matthew
Thelma
Nancy
Noel

Robert
Born
May 7th 1908
(died 1982)

Married
on
7th December 1929
Lilian Chambers Duncan
(who died 1977)

Robert
Born
6th June 1930

William (Dick) To Thora Curtains

George To Agnes Crawford

James To Betty Bell

Nancy To Alfred Ratcliffe

Malcolm
Maureen
Barry

Isabella To Albert Charlton

Violet To Stephen Foster

Other members of the Lowdon family also contributed to the provision of fresh fruit and vegetables in the home, indeed some provided removal, coal delivery and even bus hire service. Like most families in those days they were quite large. If like me you were confused as to who was related to who, then perhaps this tree kindly supplied by Bob Lowdon (the fourth generation Robert) will clarify. Sincere apologies to members of the family who are omitted.

Right: Ron Heads, Les Eltringham and Bob Lowdon (son of Lilian and Bob snr) at Princess Street, Sunniside.

Down Sunniside Road

Billy Hudspith, of Beech Street, married Margaret Rutherford, of Grange House, Streetgate on 10th July 1943. They had four children, Robert, John, Tony and Anne. He worked at Proudlocks and Swans farms before going to work at Watergate Pit. He ended his working life at Bowaters on the Team Valley. Bill died at the early age of 60 years.

Harvey and Gerard Boland of Beech Street, pictured here in the 1940s. Harvey was a very popular person with an endearing personality, his life was tragically cut short in 1997.

Bobby Hudspith (the brother of Billy) seen here at his leek trench. The two brothers were very keen gardeners and entered local leek shows with success. Bobby outlived his brother and died at the age of 74 years.

Roxburgh Cottage, Sunniside Road with Hannah Lucas (née English), *circa* 1920.

Hole Lane, (the name derives from Gellesfield Hole situated at the bottom of the lane) looking up toward Sunniside Road before the new housing was built in 1975 on the right hand side of the lane. Its interesting to note that coal mining took place at Gellesfield as long ago as 1578. Opposite the bungalow at No. 54, a shaft was sunk by George Hare of Tanfield around 1920. Dene Farm at Hole Lane was occupied in turn by, the Wallaces, Routledges and eventually Mr Sidney Easton who composed our opening monologue sometime in 1948.

Below right: Hamilton Henderson Harm, his wife Ann and son Hamilton Henderson jnr, born 1915, are pictured here in 1917. Ann was the daughter of Anne King who ran a shop at Marley Hill Hole (the Valley) around 1900. Hamilton snr became the Secretary of Sunniside Club around 1929 onward.

The younger Hamilton (who lives at Marley Hill and is now aged 83 years) married Gladys Bailey of Burnopfield, she died some time ago. They have a son also named Hamilton who now lives at Skegness.

Elsie Harm, the daughter of Hamilton and Ann, was born in 1925 at 13 Hole Lane, the family home. She served in the W.A.A.F during the Second World War. Elsie married Gordon Harley on the 5th March 1947.

Pictured here in her occupation as a dental nurse with her employer, Paul Johnson the Sunniside Dentist, is Anne Kemp. Her great-great-grandmother was Mary Brown one of the seven daughters of Anne King. Paul Johnson B.D.S. began his dental surgery at Sun Street in 1983.

Sunniside Social Club

The birth of Sunniside Club took place in a two roomed stone cottage named Rose Cottage. It was built in the late 1800s and stood on the corner where Hollywell Lane meets Sunniside Road. The owner, Pringle Appleby (1831-91) originated from Meldon to the west of Morpeth. He had started a market garden business around 1860 on one and a quarter acres of land near where Sunniside Club now stands. The land was known as Appleby Gardens and the cottage was built to house the family. After the Applebys vacated the cottage a group of local men took over in 1914 to form a Club and so began the life of one of the most important social facilities in the village and the surrounding area. In 1918, the members built a new club very close to Rose Cottage, and the cottage eventually housed the Club Steward, Ernie Robinson and his wife Mary. To allow extensions to the Club, Ernie and Mary were moved to Rose Villa, a new house built by the Club on Hollywell Lane. Rose Cottage was demolished around 1959. Ernie and Mary served the Club for many years, they were followed by Alan and Jean Gleghorn who retired in November 1997 after thirty years of service. The present Steward is Alan Gowland who came from Teams. The photograph above shows the front of the Club, it covers considerably more land to the rear.

Over the years hundreds of men have given of their time and effort to serve on the Club Committee freely and with great commitment. Pictured right on the stage in 1965 with guests, are just some of the founder members. Left to right: Joe Best, Tommy Heron, Stan Hall (Secretary Durham C.I.U.), Syd Lavers (Chairman of the Federation Brewery), Bill Liddle (Club Secretary), Bob Simpson, Rodger Henderson, Sam Treglown, Sammy Prinn, Joe Lumsdon and Victor Dillon (Club Chairman). Some of the other founder members were Hamilton Harm of Hole Lane, Tom Coulson a teacher at Marley Hill School, Bill Graham of Old Sunniside and Tom Anderson of Streetgate.

Only two Sunniside Club Officials have been elected to serve on the Board of Management at the Northern Clubs Federation Brewery. Victor Dillon from 1968 until his death in 1984 and Bill Liddle from 1989 to date, 1998. Mr Dillon attained the position of Brewery Chairman in 1974 and remained in the chair until his death.

Victor Dillon

William Liddle

The Northern Clubs Federation Brewery. The Brewery, affectionately known as 'The Fed', is owned solely by the Workingmen's Clubs, they elect the Board of Directors every year. Any Club member can be nominated to stand for election and providing they can get enough Clubs to vote for them can be elected to serve on the Board. The Brewery came into being when the private brewers priced their product out of reach of low wage earners. Thanks to people like Sunniside Club founder members, Delegates from across the region united on the 24th May 1919 at Prudhoe Club and decided to buy a Brewery. Its object would be to serve the small clubs springing up everywhere and to give them a dividend on everything they bought, much the same as the Co-op Stores. There were many obstacles but the Brewery overcame all to become a major employer, first of all at Hanover Square, Newcastle and then on to the new multi million pound premises at Dunston near the MetroCentre. The Lancastrian Suite, on the right, is a well established function room. The current Chairman is James Ramshaw who has served on the Board from June 1968. The Company has been very supportive of the Sunniside & District Local History Society since our first meeting in 1992.

MARLEY HILL

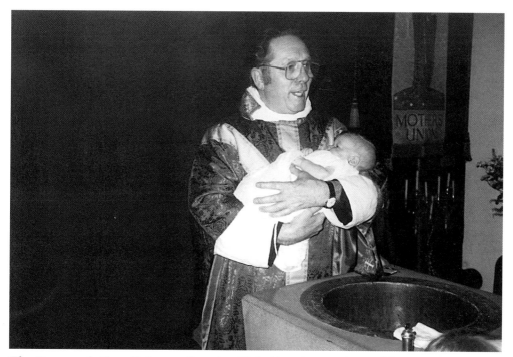

The Reverend Alan Gales performing Holy Baptism at St Cuthbert's Church.

With 31 years at Marley Hill, the longest serving Vicar of St Cuthbert's Church is Alan Gales who was born on 28th November 1929 and originated from Birtley. He trained for the Sacred Ministry at Sarum Theological College (1956-59) and was ordained into Holy Orders as Deacon on the 24th May 1959 and as a Priest on the 12th January 1960 at the Cathedral Church of Christ and the Blessed Virgin Mary at Durham. He served as Curate of Greenside (1959-60), Curate of Peterlee (1960-63), part time Industrial Chaplain (1960-70) and as Vicar of Marley Hill from 1963 until his retirement from full time Ministry on the 28th November 1994. During his years at Marley Hill Church the Reverend Gales also served as a part time Prison Chaplain (1974-81).

St Cuthbert's Church, Marley Hill
Written by Jean Mackie

St Cuthbert died on the Inner Farne Island on 20th March 687. Holy Island was his place of perfection, he loved being there. He was described as a typical Northerner; tough, warm hearted and straight to the point. His remains lie at Durham Cathedral, his original coffin, pectoral cross and vestments taken from his body, are displayed in the Cathedral treasury.

St Cuthbert's Church (above) celebrated its first Centenary on St Cuthbert's Day, Wednesday 20th March, 1974. The first Priest, Rev. Samuel White, was licensed as Minister of the Ecclesiastical District of Marley Hill on 23rd November 1874. The church was consecrated by the Bishop of Durham on 15th November 1877, whereupon the Ecclesiastical District automatically became a Parish. When St Cuthbert's was built there were many more houses nearer to the church than exist today, i.e. Old Marley Hill, Andrews House, The Hole – and consequently more people. The Church Registers date from 1868 when the area within the present Parish boundaries was recognised as a Conventional District and was served by a Priest in Charge. The church is built in the Gothic style (Gothic being the long period of architecture which existed from the twelfth to the fifteenth centuries and embodied the early English and Decorated styles. The original influence was the architecture of twelfth century France.) It cost £3,000 to build, the money being raised by public subscription. The first recorded Baptism (Herbert W. Coates) took place on 18th November 1877. (There are earlier Baptisms recorded in the register held in the Durham Archives.) The first burial (James Littleton) was on 17th December 1877 and the first marriage (William Spencer Telford and Mary Gray Thirlaway) on 16th January 1878. The first Sexton (William Howe Dye), who was killed by an accident at Marley Hill on 14th May 1880, dug graves and also rang bells. St Cuthbert's Church was licensed because of the local need for a church. Previous to this the 3 Tabernacles were at Marley Hill (where our present Church Hall is sited), Byermoor (on the field near the main road) and Sunniside (bottom of Elm Street West). They were used by worshippers and served by Vicars of neighbouring Parishes. The Churchyard was consecrated by a Bishop and is sometimes called 'God's Acre'. (Consecrated means set apart as sacred.) The Churchyard is now full and the last burial took place there on 8th October 1971. The current Priest is Stephen Radley.

The organ and lectern. The organ was constructed by Nicholson of Newcastle, *circa* 1870.

The chancel and screen. The screen separates the choir stalls from the main body of the church. On it is inscribed the names of those parishioners who lost their lives during the First World War and on the plaque behind the pulpit, those who lost their lives during the Second World War. Every Armistice Day those names are read out.

The pulpit and side altar.

The altar.

Reverend Alan Gales with his wife Myra (née Ellis) who originated from Stanley and was born 1st August 1930. They married on the 19th July 1952 and have two grown up children, Janet and Peter. The Vicar and Myra retired in 1994 and currently live at Whickham. Although officially retired the Vicar's services are still called upon occasionally.

Rev. Gales with a group of Marley Hill parishioners attending a Confirmation at Auckland Castle.

A visit to Durham Cathedral with Marley Hill parishioners with Myra Gales seeking 'sanctuary' at the Cathedral door. Left to right: Nell Armstrong, Marjorie Cranna, Myra Gales, Dorothy Oliphant, and Eleanor Woodhall.

The Church Children's Group.

Marley Hill County Primary School
Written by Joan Telford

In 1893 Marley Hill managers met at the present school site, which is about 200 yards from that which had been originally selected, and they considered it decidedly the better spot. So the new school was built by Isaac Bewley. Expenses were: cost of school, £3081; cost of house, £600; cost of fence, £80; cost of furniture, £107. The farmer who worked the field was paid £20 for the loss of his turnip crop. On completion, the building was much admired and consisted of an infant room with gallery to the rear and, facing the road, two classrooms on either side of one long room with a partition. Toilet facilities for the boys and girls were in the yard which was divided by a fence making one yard for boys and one for girls. The school was opened by Sir Charles Mark Palmer on the 1st August 1895. Sir Charles had close connections with the area. As a young man of 23, he had been in partnership with John Bowes at Marley Hill Colliery and had been responsible for the increased production of coal and coke at the pit. He was a major industrialist in the region in other fields.

A press report from Saturday, 3rd August 1895 read: 'A new Board School was opened on Thursday afternoon at Marley Hill Colliery, this being one of the institutions under the Whickham School Board. The new school will accommodate 300 children and has cost about £4,000. It was opened by Sir Charles Mark Palmer MP supported by Henry Wallace Esq, C. Berkley Esq, R. Berkley Esq, Thomas Lambert Esq and Mr Thomas Brabban, Vice-Chairman of the School Board who presided.'

Over the years the School has seen many changes, some in the form of extensions, but there has only been six Headmasters at Marley Hill School over the past hundred years: Mr Lawrence Dewhurst, Mr William Bellerby, Mr John Atkinson, Mr Robert Gardner JP, Mr Elgar Sykes and Mr Keith Rowland to date, 1998.

The current teaching staff are: Mrs Westgate, Mrs Cowen, Mrs Simpson, Ms Evitt, Mrs Partington, Mrs Doherty, Mrs Hodgson, Mr Robinson, Mr Alderson, Mr Evans, Mrs Miller, Mrs Linda Shayshutt (School Secretary) and Mr King. None teaching staff: Mrs Maddison, Mrs Wilson, Mrs Gardener, Mrs Skeen, Mrs Armstrong, Mrs Paxman and Mrs Harm the Traffic Warden. Governors: Chairman Mr Alan Ord, Vice Chair Mrs Joan Telford, Mr A. Beveridge, Mr A. Appleby, Mrs S. Gleghorn, Mr B. Dodds, Rev. S. Radley, Mr R. Kirkcaldy, Mrs P. Harris and Mrs J. Alexander. One of the longest serving non-teaching staff was Hetty Spoor (née Buglass) school dinner lady from 1949 to the mid 1970s.

A Marley Hill school class in the early 1900s. Unfortunately, the name of the teacher is unknown. The Lingey Fine Douglas triplets, May, Violet and Lily are pictured here in identical dresses – second row from the front, eighth from the left; third row from the front, fifth and sixth from the left.

A class *circa* 1920, the unkempt appearance of some of the children is heartbreaking. In an excerpt from the writings of High Row-born, Eddie Liddle, he describes the way most children were clothed in those days: 'Most of us were dressed the same, the boys wore blue ganzies (jerseys) with no collar on them and any kind of trousers in any colour, although they were always short and patched back and front so much, that it was hard to pick out the original colour. The shirts the boys wore were of a coarse grey flannel, very itchy and uncomfortable. Most of us wore no underpants or vests, our mothers couldn't afford them. In winter we suffered terribly from the frost causing chapped legs. If we wore knee length stockings they were generally hand-knitted and quite comfortable, our shorter socks were of a coarse yarn and very uncomfortable. The boys usually wore boots, hob nailed so that they would last longer, although there was nothing strange in seeing boys and girls wearing wellington boots on a hot summer's day or sandals on a cold winter's day. If anyone was lucky enough to have an overcoat for school they were generally very old and shabby, most of us wore an older brother's cast off which had been altered to fit. The girls also wore cast off clothing, some dresses were even made of sacking.'

Mr William Bell's class, *circa* 1955. Back row, left to right: Marjorie McKie, Sheila Cant, Ellen Keeble, Doreen Keenan, Margaret Palmer. Middle row: Dorothy Osborne, unknown, Anne Clapperton, Alma Newman, Muriel Armstrong, Irene Vickery. Front row: Edith Liddle, Sylvia Nixon, Eva Wilkinson, Elsie White, Honor Boyd, Margaret Ellis.

A school class in the 1950s with Mr John Atkinson, Headmaster, on the left and Mr Frank Gillender on the right.

A school class with Mr John Atkinson on the left and Mr Elgar Sykes on the right. Mr Sykes became Headmaster on the 1st December 1971.

The annual sports day on the field at the rear of the school. Some of the girls present are, Queenie Nelson, Marion Caisley, Audrey Bell, Eleanor Hurd and Dorothy Clark.

The teaching staff of 1991. Standing, left to right: Karen Dobson, Claudia Yielder and Susan Cowen. Seated: Adele Evitt, Keith Rowland, Elgar Sykes, Joan Telford (author of *The History of Marley Hill School*) and Mary Simpson. Mr Sykes retired as Headmaster in 1991 and Mr Rowland replaced him.

In 1995 the school celebrated its centenary and it was a memorable occasion for the community, especially for former pupils and teachers who returned to meet again after so many years. A group of teachers past and present are pictured here during the celebrations. Left to right: Ann Keen, Pat Valks, Jean Gaul and Mary Simpson.

Everyone participated during the centenary celebrations and staff and pupils dressed in the fashion of 100 years ago. Pictured here are just some of the staff.

Mr William Bell taught the senior class in the mid 1950s, pictured here with two former pupils, Anne Dixon (née Clapperton) and Francis G. Newman, both of whom left school in 1955.

Memories Of Old Marley Hill

Marley Hill Colliery viewed from Andrews House in April 1968. To the right can be seen the old Brockwell shaft top and the coal trucks queuing underneath the screens. Post Office Row is visible behind the shaft top. The pit closed in March 1983 and now nothing remains of that once huge industrial area. The entire site was eventually cleared and is to date, 1998, in a shameful state of neglect. No attempt has been made to tidy up or to landscape the area.

Tom English, standing between the rails, pictured in 1911 aged 19 years, was born at Granby Terrace in 1892 – the family eventually moved to live at Railway Cottage, Fugar Bar. Tom was a 'bankrider' on the gravity haulage sets of coal trucks which ran from Marley Hill Colliery to Dunston Staithes. He married Elizabeth Ann Charlton of Swalwell and they had three children, Nancy (who married David Armstrong of Peters Gates), Fred and Raymond.

The rear of Post Office Row. The pit shaft wheels can be seen above the roof of Hannah Hutchison's shop. The miners took great pride in their gardens, out of necessity they grew their own vegetables and other consumable produce. Many of them rented allotments, not only to grow produce but to keep livestock.

Middle Row, Old Marley Hill Colliery Houses, 1st March 1959. This picture shows just how close to the shaft top the houses were. The last family to live there were the Davisons. They described how conditions deteriorated over the years, with the smell becoming unbearable and some of the empty houses of Middle Row were used to stable pit ponies which also did not help the environment. The family moved out in August 1959 and the houses were demolished in 1960.

A close up view of the old Colliery Houses.

The downstairs interior of Colliery Houses. The miners received a coal allowance and so they could at least ensure a well stoked up fire. To the right, on the hearth, is the blazer, pronounced by most as 'the bleezer'. It was simply a square shaped piece of metal sheet with a handle on and when placed in front of the fire caused an upward draft which encouraged the fire to blaze. In years to come future generations will never see a live fire let alone a 'blazer' or 'fire tongs' or a 'poker'. A miner's Davey Lamp stands next to the clock on the mantelpiece and towels drape to dry off, horrifically close to the fire. The floor was stone, a cold tap was attached to the wall and there was no kitchen. A basin served as a sink and an old 'set pot' stood at the side of the fire for hot water. There was no internal drainage, dirty water had to be thrown outside and 'ash middens' outside were the only toilet.

The only upstairs room in Colliery Houses. There was an ordinary ladder just inside the door which was the only means of access to the bedroom. The lighting was by gas but most of the residents could not afford to use it, the gas mantles were expensive too and they broke very easily. Most people used candles for lighting and there was no heating in the bedroom. In cold weather a clippie mat or an overcoat had to be thrown over the blankets, an army greatcoat was a luxury.

A well furnished bedroom at Colliery Houses. Over the years improvements were made, in this picture the sloping rafters have been removed and the ceiling lifted. Just off centre of the photograph, there appears to be a ghostly figure wearing a cloak and with arm outstretched. There is no explanation for this apparition, it is certainly not a double exposure.

The last residents to vacate Colliery Houses at Old Marley Hill – the Davison family pictured in front of the pit in 1959. Left to right: Linda, Robert, Kenneth held by his father Billy, Valerie, Audrey and Joan at the back standing next to their mother Violet.

Left to right: Linda, Valerie and Joan Davison with the old Brockwell shaft top directly behind them.

Billy Davison at the shaft top just before its demolition.

Having served the community and the miners for many years, the sad sight of Hannah Hutchison's shop on Post Office Row, closed prior to demolition.

Jimmy Connelly, pictured second from the left, was stable keeper down the pit. He is seen here at a pit pony show, competing against other collieries. Second from the right is George Parkin of Marley Hill. The ponies were tended in the underground stables but they also worked shiftwork. The drivers/putters would harness their pony up and take it to the coal face. The animals worked incredibly hard and sometimes suffered injuries, some inflicted by ill-tempered putters. The closure of the mines meant the end of the exploitation of ponies, many of whom never saw daylight again after being taken below.

Meet The Community

Marley Hill Ladies. Some of those present are, Mrs Spraggon, Mrs Gowland, Mrs Thompson, Mrs Caisley, Mrs Pharoah, Mrs Mudd, Mrs Liddle and Mrs McCullaugh.

Marley Hill St Cuthbert's AFC – winners of the Northumberland & Durham League, 1907-08.

Frank Spraggon was born on 27th October 1945, he was the fourth son of William and Myra Spraggon of Marley Hill. He had three older brothers, Willie, George and Jack who all played for amateur football clubs. Jack was the youngest until Frank came along after a gap of fourteen years. With so much footballing influence around him it was inevitable that Frank would follow in his brothers' footsteps. He attended Marley Hill School and from an early age it became evident that he was a talented youngster at all sport,

excelling on the football field. At the age of eleven he transferred to Burnopfield Secondary School and was very quickly a regular in the school football team. He was joined in the team by Dave Elliott who went on to join Sunderland and later Newcastle United. Frank was selected to play for Stanley Boys and Durham County Boys at the age of fourteen. Scouts from professional clubs soon noticed the talented Spraggon and although he had spent a brief spell at Preston North End during school holidays, it was after being spotted playing for Stanley Boys at Middlesbrough that decisions about his future began to materialise. Frank was spotted by Harold Shepherdson the England and Middlesbrough trainer who went on to become the England trainer for more than 100 games including the 1966 World Cup. Harold took a more important role in Frank's life, becoming his father-in-law when his daughter, Linda married him in 1968. In 1960, at the age of fifteen, Frank joined Middlesbrough Football Club as an apprentice professional and played for them until the 1975-76 season. He played his last game against Derby County in the First Division. During those years he had played under four managers, Bob Dennison, Raich Carter, Stan Anderson and Jack Charlton. Although a knee operation and a damaged optic nerve threatened to end Frank's career at the age of twenty-six, he went on to play for the Boro team which won promotion in 1974. Frank left the Boro having played 300 first team games and he went on to join the North American Soccer League Club, Minnesota Kicks. After spending six months in the USA and having played against the world's best, including Pele, Eusebio, George Best, Rodney Marsh and Bobby Moore, a knee injury ended Frank's career at the age of thirty. A fully qualified FA coach, as pictured above, Frank has spent his time coaching youngsters at home and abroad since his playing career ended. He is currently employed by his old club Middlesbrough, working for their Football Academy with local youngsters aspiring to become Boro's stars of the future.

Frank Spraggon playing against the legendary Brazilian, Pele.

Marley Hill CW Football Club, *circa* 1960. Back row, left to right: A. Liddle, E. Charlton, unknown, E. Swinburne, R. Ridler, unknown, J. Pearson, J. Taskas. Front row: S. Grant, R. Croft, R. Davidson, I. Marsham, E. Reay.

Bobby Chisholm played for Marley Hill AFC in 1910.

Girls from the three villages at Blackpool, *circa* 1956. In the front seats, Frances Clifton and Nancy Finlay. Sitting behind, left to right: Betty Heron, Maureen Mitchell, Kathleen Ratcliffe and her sister Margaret.

Percy Mitchell in typical pose (Lord of the Manor), pipe in mouth and walking stick in hand. A former coal miner and a very popular character.

Freda McCullaugh with her sister Jean and Avril and David Johnson, outside the Pre-fabs at Marley Hill in 1951.

High Row

An extract from the diary of Eddie Liddle, born 14th February 1909, died 25th July 1982.

Life begins for all of us in many varied ways, mine began at High Row. This was a one street place, one could hardly call it a village as there was no church or pub. There was a small shop, if it could qualify for that name, a Mrs Ellison kept it. I can remember that it sold sweets, tobacco, mineral waters, boiled ham, corned beef, boot laces, pins, cotton and I often spent my pennies and half-pennies there. It had no shop window as we know them today, it was just the same kind of house as the rest of the street. In each house there were two attic bedrooms, a large living room, a cold slab pantry you could walk into, which was something like the kitchenettes of modern times. There was also a front room called the parlour (the best room). This very often had to act as a bedroom and would have a double bed with brass fittings. Unfortunately some of the houses only had two bedrooms, this included the 'parlour' downstairs. There was no front door because these were back to back houses and most of those were at the top end of the street, I think I was born in one of those. However, we left there before I was old enough to remember much. I was very fond of High 'Raar' as we used to call it, my favourite relatives lived there, Aunt Vinnie and Uncle Thomas James. I became very fond of those two over the years. We left High Row to move into the new houses with Granddad Liddle at 19 Cuthbert Street, I am not sure when grandmother died. We were close to a church named St Cuthbert's, there were two shops, again in ordinary houses. One in Cuthbert Street was ran by a Mrs Joe Clark, on the even numbered side and nearer to us was the other shop. It was ran on more elaborate lines and even sold wet fish, a most welcome commodity. The houses were better than High Row, some better than others. The best ones had two bedrooms, a living room, a scullery, a large pantry and even a bath. They also had a front garden, but all houses had a back yard with an earth toilet 'the closet' and next to that a coal house. In our house lived Granddad, Mother, Father, brothers Bill, Joe, Tommie, sister Dorrie and of course myself. Because we had only two bedrooms we had to have a double bed in the living room. With the large families of those days almost everyone had to do the same thing.

Joseph Robson Liddle with his wife Sarah Jane (née Prinn). They married on 30th May 1899 and were the parents of Eddie Liddle, who wrote such a detailed account of his boyhood days at High Row and Marley Hill.

The Vickery family of High Row. Left to right: Sarah Jane, Caroline, William, Elizabeth, Ellen (became Nelly Rolfe), Lena Edith with Louisa centre front.

Sarah Jane Vickery, born 1855.

William Vickery, born 1851.

Caroline Vickery, born around 1872.

The anomalies in relationships created by large families is illustrated with this photograph of William Brown, born 1872 at High Row, and his Aunt Sarah Jane Vickery.

William Brown, *circa* 1902.

William Vickery at High Row in later years beside his greenhouse.

Thomas James Taskas of High Row cobbling his shoes, a common sight in the old days.

Esther (Grannie) Gibson of 34 High Row. At the age of 17 years she was the first foot passenger on the Armstrong Bridge at Newcastle. She was born at Seghill and moved to High Row when she got married. Her husband was a 'Sinker' (the men who sank the pit shafts) in the coal mines, he showed her how to pack a pipe and she smoked for 53 years. They had eight children, Isabelle, Margaret, Esther, Sally, Frances, Eina, Joe and William. Grannie was the head of five generations and lived until the great age of 95 years. She had lived at Marley Hill for 68 years.

Coal miners of Marley Hill, *circa* 1900, carrying their oil-filled midgey lamps.
Standing second from the right is Thomas James Taskas of High Row
(a Cornishman by birth). Third and fourth from the right are his cousins.

Lavinia Taskas (née Prinn),
Esther Taskas (centre) and
Tommy Taskas at High Row.

Thomas James Taskas and son, Tommy,
who was known as Bud.

The Causey

Amelia Boyd (née Allan), 1886-1981, and her husband Robert Boyd, 1886-1941. They moved to the Causey in 1939. At one time Robert operated the barriers at Peters Gates then he moved on to operate a signal box further on up the line. They had four daughters and five sons, Margaret, Isobel, Mildred, Doris, Bill, Alan, Robert, Frank and Colin. No family contributed more during two World Wars than the Boyds, some of the family will feature later in the book.

The original Bankwell House at the Causey. Underground mining tunnels caused the house to subside and become uninhabitable. The family built a new house nearby, it is currently owned by Colin and Lillian Boyd.

Isobel Seager (née Boyd) sitting on the gate of the original Bankwell House.

Colin Boyd (born 18th April 1926) married Lillian Harris on 26th May 1947. They live at Bankwell House, the Causey and to date have three grown-up daughters, two sons, fourteen grandchildren and one great-grandson. Colin is pictured here with Lillian on his left, his sister Isobel on his right and niece Isobel Boyd (daughter of Alan) in front.

Working on Bankwell Farm. Colin Boyd, driving the tractor, farmed from being very young, eventually he became a tenant farmer then owner. He specialised in cattle, pigs and poultry. Pictured here with him are, in the foreground, left to right, Alan Strong, Philip Walker and young Colin Boyd. Standing at the back is Wilf Graham.

The children of the Causey School, 1944. Back row, left to right: Noel Palmer, Boysy Thompson, Alec Bainbridge (who went on to receive a Doctorate in Botany), Alan Seager (who became a ship's captain and pilot) and Jim Laybourne. Unfortunately, in the middle row the only girl known is Jenny Foster, of Parkhead Farm, in the centre. Front row: Maurice Abbot (became the butcher for Reed's at Sunniside), Bruce Robson (became a veterinary) Angus Gardener, Douglas Watson, of the Causey Inn, and Eddie Handy.

Andrews House

Mrs Crosson of Bowes Terrace.

Mrs Mary Anne Bell and her daughters Maimi and Isabel.

High Marley Hill

The celebration bonfire built by local people for the Coronation of George V in 1911. The little lad in the centre holding the kite is Bob Craig who used to live at Prospect Terrace, Sunniside. He was destined to marry Lily Douglas, one of the Lingey Fine triplets.

BYERMOOR TO THE HOBSON

The Byermoor Colliery Banner 1872

Success to every Union
And everyone that's true;
Now we're bound together,
Lets try what we can do,
Our masters they do tell us,
That if we mean to stand,
We shall do ourselves an injury
And the trade will leave the land
But in that we have advantage,
And that you know is true;
For if the trade leaves England,
We can leave it too.

Byermoor Colliery Closed 31st January 1968.

1872 - 160 Collieries in Durham
1996 -   0 Collieries in Durham

Robin Oliphant of Byermoor standing on the pit heap. The photograph shows the full colliery site and many of the old Colliery Houses. The church and school can be seen on the skyline. This is one of the few existing photographs to show the area including the colliery.

Byermoor Sacred Heart School
Written by Sheila McGahon

Following the construction of the first temporary church in 1869, Father Mathews, the Parish Priest, began the establishing of education for the children of the Parish. The church building was combined to share services and formal schooling. On the 4th March 1871 teaching began, with a total of 48 pupils attending and the number gradually increasing throughout the following years. Pupils had to pay for their lessons, the charges being: Standard One, 2d per week and Standards Two – Six, 3d per week. In that same year there was an outbreak of small-pox at the school.

A number of certificated teachers took charge, they were aided by assistants and girls

Byermoor School staff in the 1950s. Back row, left to right: Mr Frank Doran, Mr James Kehoe (Headmaster) and Mr Eric Smith. Front row: Miss Winifred Clark, Miss Clare Arnold, Father Austin Pickering and Miss Alice Kehoe (the Headmaster's sister).

who were paid to act as monitresses. Figures show that a total of ten teachers and two monitresses served at the school between 1871-83. Miss Blanche Lamb of Gibside Hall and Miss Elizabeth Surtees of Hamsterley Hall often visited the school and distributed sweets and held parties for the children. In 1876, following the building of the new church, the old building was then used solely as a school. In 1880 it was recorded that the number of pupils now totalled 164. On 14th October 1881 tragedy struck, following a violent storm in

Byermoor School Class 2, *circa* 1910. Cissie Young is on the right side of the middle row with a ribbon in her hair.

which the wind had battered the school, the whole wooden structure collapsed and was totally destroyed. It was said at the time that two main doors had been left open and the wind had swept through the building with disastrous results

The outcome was, the children now had to take lessons in the new Church. Shortly afterwards work commenced on the building of a new school and two houses on the edge of the main Newcastle road. One house was for the Headmaster and the other for the school caretaker. On 5th January 1883 the new Roman Catholic School at Byermoor was formally opened. It had been built at a cost of £1600. One of the benefactors was the Marquis of Bute and an average of 150 children

Pictured here in March 1994, on the left, is Miss Clare Arnold, the extremely popular former Deputy Head at Byermoor School. She taught there for forty-five years and retired in 1976. On the right is Miss Sheila McGahon who spent thirty-one years in the schools' meals service, she retired in 1991.

attended the school. In 1905 the school was enlarged to three classrooms and one room big enough to use for two classes. The girls' and boys' playgrounds (yards), were divided by sheds. In the girls' shed a stove was kept, this was used by them to keep their cans of tea warm. Children walked long distances to school in those days, some from Sunniside, Andrews House, Marley Hill, Burnopfield, Leazes, Tanfield and Rowlands Gill. Life at the school flourished, the children were given a good grounding in religious and academic studies, with lots of activities. School concerts were very popular and from the 1920s the girls attended cookery classes at High Marley Hill Board School. They were given excellent tuition in the art of domestic science. The boys attended weekly woodwork classes at the school in Burnopfield.

Pictured in the centre, on sports day at the school, is Mrs Margaret Sands the current Head Teacher.

Down the years, Byermoor School produced many good football teams and kept a good record in other sporting activities, winning a number of honours including cups and medals when competing against other schools. A number of its former pupils went on to become professional footballers at top football clubs. James McConnon became a well-known test cricketer and played for England on a number of occasions, his home team was Glamorgan. This excellent little school, with its dedicated teaching staff, has throughout the years played its part in the formation, both educationally and morally, of the characters of its past pupils.

Year six of Byermoor School pupils.

Head Teachers of Byermoor School over the years: Mr Nicholas Kelly, Mr Daniel Henry, Mr Matthew White, Mr Matthew Coleman, Mr James Kehoe, Mr Henry Gardner, Mr Anthony Hannon, Miss Kim Bradley (acting Head Teacher) and currently Mrs Margaret Sands.

The Reception Class at Byermoor School.

Byermoor School football team. Back row, left to right: Mr Kehoe (Headmaster), Leo Nash, Joe O'Rourke, Tony Doran, Billy Hall, John Hanratty, Tom Smith. Front row: Paul O'Rourke, Billy Cranney, Tom Carrick, Derek Armstrong, John McCormick.

Tom Carrick (born 28th October 1940) played football at Byermoor until 1951 when he moved to Annfield Plain Secondary Modern. He played for their school team from 1951-56 as well as playing for the District Under 11s at Byermoor. He played for the County at Annfield Plain Secondary Modern and after leaving school played for Annfield Plain

Tom Carrick in 1952, aged twelve years.

Right: Tom Carrick, on the left, with Billy Hall – both played for the District.

Juniors and then signed for Sunderland AFC. He went to Luxembourg with the England youth team and eventually left Sunderland in 1961 to play for Scarborough. After three years he returned to play for Annfield Plain senior team and ended his playing career with them.

John Edward Craggs was born at Flint Hill, 31st October 1948. Throughout his years at school he was encouraged to play football by the Headmaster, Harry Gardner. He signed as an apprentice for Newcastle United in 1964 and played for them until 1971. He won a Fairs Cup medal in 1969 and remembers especially the match played in a blizzard against Vittoria Setubal – Newcastle won that game 5-1. John achieved international honours when he played for the England youth team. He was transferred to Middlesbrough in 1971 and played for them for eleven years. He returned to Newcastle in 1982 and played his last game there on 30th April 1983. During his career he played alongside some famous names, probably the most noteworthy being Kevin Keegan. The most difficult person he ever

Byermoor School Football Team, 1956-57. Back row, left to right: John Hinds, John Craggs, Andrew Graham, Kevin McMahon, Tom Hall. Front row: Kevin Lowdon, Peter McMahon, John Humble, Harry McMahon, Kevin Joyce, Kenneth Gordon. The teacher is Mr Eric Smith.

played against was George Best. John is married to Denise and they have two children, Steven and Sharon. During his distinguished career he played over sixty games for Newcastle United and 409 games for Middlesbrough.

John Craggs returned to Byermoor School to present prizes in July 1969.

Byermoor Sacred Heart Church, pictured shortly after the building of the Presbytery in 1882.

Father Austin Pickering with George Joyce on the left and Billy McMahon, the handyman, on the right. Father Pickering replaced Father Chadwick on 21st February 1925 and began at once to establish a number of church societies and organisations for a range of age groups. The SVP were already in place, the Boy Scouts were formed in 1927, the Catholic Women's League in 1931, and the Girl Guides in 1936. Other popular groups were the Children of Mary, Knights of St Columba, Catholic Young Men's Society and, in 1955, the Legion of Mary was the last society to be formed. During the hard times of the 1926 General Strike, Father Pickering organised a soup kitchen at the school where families received free meals. All manner of fund raising activities took place to raise funds to buy leather for repairing the children's footwear – the local men carried out the work. On 17th May 1930, after many years of petitioning, Harry Kindred, a local builder, began work on the Church Hall. It was opened by Bishop Thorman on 27th September 1930. In 1941 Father Pickering bought a large wooden hut from the Boys' Club at Marley Hill, it was erected near the Parish Hall and became known as the Youth Hut. Between 1953-59, Father John McKeown used to travel to Byermoor at weekends to assist Father Pickering in his duties. In 1960 Father Wilfred Wright was appointed as Curate of the Parish, he served in that position for eight years. Father Pickering reached the great age of 87 years and after a prolonged period of ill health he died on 24th April 1968. He was greatly respected by people of all denominations, having served the Parish for 43 years he was a great loss. The Church Processions were very special to Father Pickering, the following photographs of the children in processions illustrate why.

Clare Hagan, centre, with Genevieve Young to her right, *circa* 1953.

Mary Dwyer, May Queen, with Father Pickering and other children, *circa* 1942.

May Queen Aileen Joyce, *circa* 1943. The little lad carrying the crown is Peter Hagan.

Kevin Joyce was born on 9th September 1947 and he was described by everyone who knew him as a lovely little lad. On 17th May 1957, in a tragic accident on a nearby railway line, Kevin lost his life. The accident, which shocked and saddened the entire community, illustrated the dangers faced by the children in those days, who lived so close to the mining industry and all it entailed.

May Queen Mary Dwyer, with Peggy Snaith leading the procession.

West Farm Byermoor

Evelyn Callaghan of Byermoor with West Farm behind her.

Grace Brown, of West Farm, with her daughters Cissie and Grace (who married Edward Clark of Marley Hill).

Walter Brown of West Farm, pictured here with his cart. He used to sell ice cream around the area.

Nobody seems to know why the two houses were given the title of 'farm'. There is little information available but apparently the pit ponies were stabled to their rear. In a passageway in the rearmost of the houses, the canaries belonging to the pit were caged. In the years before the availability of the gas detecting Davey Lamp, canaries were taken to the coal face, if they keeled over the miners would leave the area with great haste. The houses were very close to the school, lying directly between it and the last house on Gibside Crescent. They were demolished around 1950.

Byermoor Council Houses
Written by Sheila McGahon

As the population grew in the area, there was a need for a greater volume of houses and for improved conditions within them. On 12th August 1920 a letter was despatched from the Whickham Urban District Council to the Minister of Health, asking for approval of tenders received by the Council from local builders, to commence the building of twenty-five pairs of houses on land at Byermoor. On 14th October a contract was authorised with the seal of approval from the Council. It was awarded to Sunniside builder, Mr Harry Kindred for the construction of fifty houses at

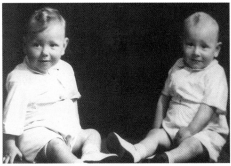

Twins Ronnie and Joseph Callaghan of Council Houses, born 5th July 1943. Joe died in May 1994.

Byermoor. In the Council Minutes book dated 14th October 1920, it is recorded that a motion was proposed by Councillor Lennox, that the Clerk be instructed to apply to the Ministry of Health, for sanction to borrow from the Public Works Loan Board, the sum of £40,309 for the building of the fifty houses. The work commenced in September 1920. In July 1921 plans were submitted by Messrs John Bowes & Partners for the proposed erection of three houses at Byermoor to house Colliery Officials (later a fourth house was erected). These plans were approved by the Council. The houses were built a little apart from the Council Houses and are now privately owned.

By May 1922 the Council Houses were being occupied and by December 1922 all of the houses were occupied. The houses consisted of three bedrooms, a toilet and bathroom, a sitting room, living room and small kitchen, with some living rooms having two single windows and others having one double. The first rents were charged at 22/- (£1.10) inclusive of rates per week, for the five roomed houses. At first the houses were known only as the Council Houses, then in October 1923, faced with a continued housing shortage, the Council allowed sub-letting of the houses. On 1st April 1924, at a Council meeting, the surveyor reported that the houses at Byermoor had been numbered in Crescents and suggested that they be named as follows: Strathmore, Bowes, Ravensworth and Gibside. The names of course were very well known in the area and were accepted without hesitation. These houses were later named 'Dolly Town'. There are two versions of the origins of the

The Handy sisters, Evelyn, Ellen, Florrie, Margaret and Annie, with friends Florrie and Alice Nicholson.

name, one being that they resembled dolls houses. The other that when the Council allowed sub-letting, there were a good number of children, mostly girls. Therefore there was always a large number of dolls on display when they played, neither explanation seems very likely.

The People of Byermoor

John Patrick (Jack) Callaghan (born 9th August 1907, died 1968) with his wife Evelyn (born 18th November 1904, died 1988).

John Patrick and Margaret Callaghan with their dog Judy, on Marley Hill Church bank.

Sarah Jane Handy reached the great age of 84 years. She is pictured here with Ronny Warnaby, Evelyn Callaghan and Margaret Callaghan in the centre.

Mary Dwyer at the Council Houses.

The Joyce Family

Grandfather James Joyce.

Grandmother Mary Joyce.

Margaret Joyce, pictured in January 1917, married Michael Dwyer. They had three children, Mary, Joseph and Monica.

James Joyce originated from Connemara, County Galway on the west coast of Ireland. He had two brothers, Larry and Harry and two sisters, Mary and Margaret. In 1884 he met and married Mary Lamb who was aged eighteen years. She had come to England as a child, from Dundalk on the north east coast of Ireland. Her parents were Peter and Julia Lamb who had two other daughters, Julia and Anne and a son Peter. James and Mary settled in the north east of England, first at Andrews House then on to Marley Hill and finally Byermoor. They had thirteen children in total but only eight survived, they were: Harry, born 1888, Anne, 1891-1960, (she was a dinner lady at Byermoor school for many years), Larry, 1893-1959, Meggy, 1895-1982, Michael, 1899-1962, Austin, 1901-66, George, 1903-53 (never married) and James, 1905-82. Grandfather James Joyce died in 1935 and Grandmother Mary Joyce died in 1953, at the age of 87 years. They had nineteen grandchildren in total and at one stage there was a branch of the Joyce family in all four Crescents of Byermoor.

Michael Joyce.

Lawrence and Elizabeth Joyce (née Carter).

Alice Joyce (née Marron) of Harelaw, married James Joyce in 1935

Left to right: Kate Dunphy, Anne Joyce, Elizabeth Etherington and Meggie (Margaret) Joyce.

Friends Austin Ratcliffe, on the left, and Joseph Dwyer whose mother was formerly a Joyce. Pictured here on 15th May 1948.

Grandma Joyce with just some of her grandchildren.

Grandma Joyce with Aileen, at the back, Helen, on the left and Margaret.

Anne Joyce (who was school dinner lady and known to all as Aunty Anne) with her nieces, Kathleen, Anne and Margaret.

Grandma Joyce with granddaughters, Margaret Mary, on the left, and Margaret.

Gerard, aged seven years, and Kevin Joyce, aged three years, pictured here in August 1951.

Kevin Joyce with his sister Anne (centre) and her friend Margaret Ratcliffe.

Byermoor People Past And Present

Left to right: Billy Eddy, Jackie Porter and David Young in the 1960s. The three worked at Marley Hill Colliery.

Byermoor people, like all close-knit communities in bygone days, often organised a trip to the seaside. Pictured here around 1950, on such a trip are a number of well known names. Some who are sadly no longer with us are, Evelyn Callaghan, Essie Shutt, Hilda Clifton, Anne Kilkenny, Mary Ratcliffe and Joannah Campbell. The children in the foreground are, Margaret Ratcliffe (digging in the sand), Genevieve Young, Andrew Graham, the little lad standing (died in November 1997, aged 52 years) and Hillary Phelps.

Fred and Jenny Stephenson were the first tenants of Byermoor Council Houses. They were twins, born on 25th February 1911, they never married, choosing to stay together all of their lives. Jenny worked for many years as Caretaker at Marley Hill Board School, she was the older by 30 seconds and always maintained that the two of them had never had an argument. Fred, who to date is still alive, was once a boxer and a coal miner. He told of how he had T.T.F. branded into the shaft of his coal hewer's pick, this was to remind him to 'Take your Time Freddie'. *The Evening Chronicle* had a full page story on the twins to celebrate their 85th birthday in 1996. Sadly within a matter of weeks the newspaper had to report that Jenny had died.

Gracie Rix of Strathmore Crescent, her husband Arthur was a coal miner who cobbled footwear for neighbours as a sideline. They had two daughters, Grace and Eileen and a son Jack. Grace married and went to Holland, Eileen now lives at Leadgate, Jack emigrated.

Eva Gooch of Strathmore Crescent. She married John Doran. Her brother, Alan, married John's sister, Lillian.

Pat McGahon, aged fourteen years, pictured at Byermoor Council Houses in 1935. He died on 30th December 1992.

Latvian, Zanis Neilands left his native land during the Second World War. He and his fellow countrymen were forced to fight for the German Army when Latvia was invaded. To escape the turmoil they fled to England where they were based at Hamsterley Hall as 'Displaced Persons'. He eventually met and married the widowed Mary Ratcliffe in 1965. He remained at Gibside Crescent, Byermoor until his death on 11th December 1990.

Margaret Anne Young.

Jack Young (Margaret's son) married Winifred Kilkenny. They had two sons, David and Michael and two daughters, Anne and Genevieve.

Cissie Wright (née Young, daughter of Margaret pictured above) married John Wright and is pictured here with her son John.

William Kilkenny (born 24th July 1922) became an Electronics Engineer and worked for A.E.I. travelling all over the country installing telephone exchanges. He died on 1st January 1975 following a relatively short illness.

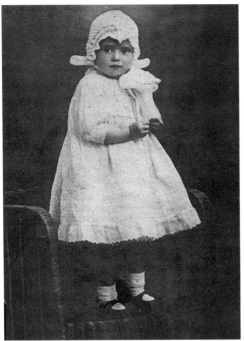

Kathleen Kilkenny was born 30th November 1914 at Colliery Houses, Byermoor. She moved to London following the death of her father in the mid 1930s. Kathleen died on 19th February 1977.

Pictured here in 1929, Kathleen Kilkenny, in front, with Nelly Mulcahy (became Boland) on the right, unfortunately the name of the other young lady is not known to us. The three worked at Blackburn's Chemist at Burnopfield.

John Patrick (Jack) Callaghan of Byermoor, enjoying a pint at the Pack Horse Inn, Crookgate. The pub was much smaller in years gone by with the door facing the main Byermoor to Burnopfield road. It was a favourite 'watering hole' for generations of Byermoor coal miners and also did a roaring trade on Sundays, when the parishioners left church.

The Hobson

A long forgotten sight, photographed in April 1968 by enthusiast Trevor Ermel, the level crossing at Crookgate Bank top, closed to allow a steam engine through with coal trucks filled at the Hobson pit. Byermoor Colliery Houses can be seen in the background.

The Hobson Colliery photographed in April 1968 by Trevor Ermel. It shows the pit in full production, it closed in July 1968.

At the Hobson pit, around 1966, without warning the earth opened up near the stables swallowing up a pit pony named Jack. It was caused by a cave in of a mining tunnel below the surface. Although the pony sank to a depth of about twenty feet, miners were able to bring Jack to the surface uninjured. Pictured here are some of the miners, many of them not in their work clothes, having either finished their shift or prior to changing for their oncoming shift. The man on the right of the group, hauling on the pulley ropes and wearing a white shirt, is Anty Scott who lived on Front Street.

The pony is steadily reaching the surface and seems remarkably calm. The men risked their lives during this act of great compassion. The ground may have opened up even further.

Safe at last and at home. Jack with miner Walter Hall. The pony seems none the worse following its ordeal.

The Hobson Colliery Band in the early 1900s.

The First Burnopfield Carnival Committee, 1933.

The Hobson People

Standing, left to right: Nelly Sowerby (née Ratcliffe), Mary Ratcliffe (née Lake) and Mr and Mrs Alfy Powell. In front are Jimmy and Alfy Ratcliffe.

The Sowerby Family. Standing, left to right: Robert and wife Mary, John, Jacky, Joan and husband Jimmy. Sitting: John jnr, Nelly (née Ratcliffe) and Betty.

We featured in our previous book, the people of Marley Hill and Sunniside arranging concerts to entertain the community in the days before in-house entertainment. The following photographs show the people of the Hobson and Burnopfield on stage at the Hobson Chapel. There is no better example of the way communities have been broken down since those gentler days, than the fact that the Hobson Chapel is no longer a place of worship or a focal point for the community. The Chapel still stands and is currently occupied by a building and D.I.Y. company.

No professional theatrical company could have paid as much attention to detail as this amateur group. Their costumes and the manner of their positioning, portrays the fact that many hours of rehearsal must have taken place.

It says much for the community spirit which existed in those days, that from a relatively small population, enough enthusiasm could be generated to persuade so many people to take part in a production. Fifty-six people throng the stage, all portraying a happy and close-knit community, something which is sadly lacking today.

Robert Ratcliffe who had sons Jack, Bob, Harry, Jimmy, Alfy and one daughter Nelly, who married John Sowerby.

Betty Sowerby and her nephew John.

Joan (née Ratcliffe) and Sid Gamble with their twin children, Jacqueline and Gillian.

Alfred on the left, and his brother Jimmy Sowerby. Alfred sadly died at a very young age.

Robert Sowerby (right), was born on 3rd July 1922 at Waggon Hill Farm, Pickering Nook. At the age of six months his family moved to Moyles Terrace, the Hobson. They lived there for almost sixteen years, then the family moved to Chapel Street. Robert was educated at Pickering Nook until he was eleven years old, then moved to Burnopfield Intermediate. He was one of the first pupils at Burnopfield when it opened after the summer of 1933. He left school at fourteen years of age and went to work at the Hobson pit but left there to train as a joiner in the building trade. He attended the Hobson Chapel when Reverend Goodacre was the Minister, the Reverend Thompson followed him. Robert was also a member of the Boys' Brigade which was ran by Alex Stevenson and Bill Hogg. He met Mary Barron, a Dipton girl, and they eventually married in 1944 at St  James' Church. Robert, Mary and the rest of the Sowerby family took an active part in the community, taking part in the Chapel concerts was one of their interests. Mary was also a member of the Mothers' Union for forty years. Robert and Mary began married life at Hill Top, Dipton and live there to this day. They have one son John and two grandchildren.

Robert Sowerby with his son John at Chapel Street.

Mary and Robert Sowerby.

In winter, travelling from the relatively low area of Watergate up to the Hobson and beyond, used to be like travelling from one continent to another. The snow getting deeper and deeper, with conditions progressively worsening, particularly from High Marley Hill onward. What would be a mild snowstorm at Watergate became a howling blizzard at the Hobson. The following photographs, taken in the bitter winter of 1963, illustrate just how severe the winters were in the past. Those who hold the opinion that there has been no significant climatic change over the years and that there is no such thing as 'the greenhouse effect', should consider the severity of the elements of yesteryear, so graphically depicted in these photographs of the Hobson.

The road to Pickering Nook.

Mason Terrace with drifts piled at least 15 feet high.

The bus stop temporarily out of action.

Jim Scott, of Front Street, dwarfed by the drifts.

Front Street, looking toward the top of the Hobson/Crookgate bank.

A bulldozer stuck in the snow at the Hobson Hotel. The first four houses in the distance are still Front Street. The first building facing the camera was a Post Office called Moss House with the Post Mistress' house next door called Mile End House.

Many of the original houses no longer exist, in those days the Front Street houses were better known as Canary Row. Mason Row stood where the golf club stands now, they were the houses allocated to minor officials at the pit, generally known as the 'Keekers'. Chapel Street and West Street ran from the Chapel toward the railway lines and pit, that site is now an industrial estate. Bowes Terrace (Low Rows) back to back streets were adjacent to the pit and the pit baths. The Under-Manager of the pit lived at Bowesville near the Fell bank top, where the edge of the golf course is now.

A Glimpse of Burnopfield

Just down the bank from the Hobson, Burnopfield was the major shopping centre for the surrounding area including Byermoor. There was a Co-op Store on the front street with the various departments in different buildings which attracted a lot of custom. Although there was a small Co-op at the Fell the larger store at Burnopfield offered a wider range of goods, and of course there was the very popular 'store dividend' to accumulate. When the Grand Cinema was open it was also the main entertainment facility in the locality.

Right: Tommy and Ethel Hudspith. They ran a General Dealers shop on the front street of Burnopfield.

Tommy Hudspith at work in his shop on 10th February 1954. Tommy was a very popular man especially with the children who called to buy sweets. Sadly the huge shopping precincts springing up everywhere are gradually leading to the closure of most of the 'corner shops', so popular in years gone by. We can end our journey with this picture of Tommy happily at work, the old cash register and scales on the counter and the jars of sweets, are unfortunately like many other things becoming relics of the past. But we still have our memories and nobody can ever take those away.

SECTION FIVE

REMEMBER THE BLESSINGS

We met and we married a long time ago
We worked for long hours when wages were low
No TV, no wireless, no bath, times were hard
Just cold water taps and a walk up the yard.
No holidays abroad, no posh carpets on floors
But we had coal on the fire, and we didn't lock doors.
Our children arrived, no pill in those days
And we brought them all up, without any state aid.
They were quite safe to go out and into the park
And old folk could also go out in the dark.
No valium, no drugs, no LSD
We cured most of our ills with a nice cup of tea.
But if you were sick you were treated at once
No fill in a form and come back in six months.
No vandals, no muggings, there was nothing to rob
And we were quite rich with a couple of bob.
People were happier in those far off days
Kinder and caring in so many ways.
Milkmen and paperboys used to whistle and sing
A night at the pictures was having a fling.
We all got our share of trouble and strife
And we just had to face it, that's the pattern of life.
But now I look back through the years
I don't think of the hard times, the trouble, the tears.
I remember the blessings, our home, our love
And that we shared them together
I thank God up above.

Everyone Enjoys A Good Wedding

In this modern era even the sanctity of marriage is attacked as old fashioned and outdated. For those of us who do still value the commitment of marriage, we hope that this section will bring back happy memories and delight those who spot friends or relatives. For those who are fashion conscious, the changes which have taken place over the decades are illustrated in this array of pictures.

Right: What better photograph to start with than Bob and Jennie (née Storey) Crosson of Sunniside celebrating their Golden Wedding Anniversary, 50 years together as a devoted couple.

Michael Dwyer and Margaret Joyce in the 1920s.

Fred McCullaugh and Evelyn Ashton were married at St Cuthbert's Church, Marley Hill in November 1935.

The friends and family of Lily Douglas (of the Lingey Fine triplets) and Bob Craig who were married on the 23rd June 1928.

Elsie Harm of Hole Lane, Sunniside married Gordon Harley, 5th March 1947. Theirs was a true wartime romance, they met in the N.A.A.F.I. Club at Newcastle. Gordon was from a South Shields seafaring family and breaking with family tradition he served with Montgomery's famous 'Desert Rats'. Fifty-one years later, they are still together and live at Gosforth. (Elsie is also featured on page 44).

The wedding day of Ned Boland of Sunniside and Jenny Laybourne. On the left is Mick Boland and on the right Rita Todd.

The marriage of Eleanor Ashton to Leslie Brown at St Cuthbert's Church, November 1946. The bridesmaids in the front are, Freda McCullaugh and Stephanie Heads.

The happy couple are Joe Handy of Byermoor and Beryl. They were married on 15th February 1947 and the best man was Sep Jennings of Colliery Houses.

The wartime wedding of Kathleen Kilkenny of Byermoor and Stan Hunter from London, 1st January 1944.

The wedding of Byermoor-born Billy Ratcliffe to Mary Greener on 30th July 1955.

Austin Ratcliffe of Byermoor married Sylvia Newton on 20th March 1954.

The wedding day of Ronnie Musgrove of the Hobson and Kathleen Ratcliffe of Byermoor on 29th December 1956.

Frances Boyd of Sunniside (daughter of Robert the Cobbler) married Joe Johnson in 1946.

Ernie Boyd (the brother of Frances pictured above) married Joyce Rutherford on 9th October 1948.

Ronnie Warnaby of Byermoor and
Eileen Trotter of Dipton on their
wedding day, 15th July 1953.

Freda McCullaugh and Leonard
Hodgson at St Cuthbert's Church,
Marley Hill, May 1961.

Edith Johnston, the daughter of Reed's
butcher Jack and his wife Esther, was
born 29th July 1945. She lived in
Sunniside until after her marriage in
1970. In 1968 she was staying with a
friend Judith Young (née Burns) a
former Sunniside girl, at Lippstadt in
West Germany. Judith's husband was in
the Armed Forces and a local pub 'The
Long Bar' was a popular place for
Servicemen. It was there on a night out
on 10th August that Edith met her
husband to be, Jim Reid. Jim was a
Serviceman and according to Edith
quiet natured, the exact opposite to her.
Six months later his regiment returned
to England and on 7th February 1969
Jim and Edith got engaged. Jim is a
Scotsman, born on 15th March 1939 in
Dunfermline, he joined the Royal
Artillery in July 1959. He served in

Cyprus, Libya, Germany and Northern Ireland and attained the rank of a
Senior N.C.O. Edith and Jim married at Sunniside Methodist Chapel on 7th
February 1970, exactly one year after their engagement. Following a serious
injury whilst on duty, Jim was medically discharged from the Army. Although
he retains his Scottish accent he is now as much a 'Sunnisider' as anyone else.
A popular character he is very active in the community. They have two
daughters April and Gaile, a son Cameron and a granddaughter Carla.

SECTION SIX

ON THE FRONT LINE

A Soldier stood at the Pearly Gate,
His face was scarred and old.
He stood before the man of fate
For admission to the fold.
'What have you done,' St Peter asked,
'To gain admission here?'
'I've been a Soldier, sir,' he said,
'For many and many a year.'
The Pearly Gate swung open wide
As St Peter touched the bell.
'Inside,' he said, 'and choose your harp,
You've had your share of hell.'

Thiepval War Memorial in France.

After the First World War the remains of hundreds of British and
Commonwealth Soldiers, some from this area, were never recovered. Their
names are engraved on the faces of this memorial erected by the War Graves
Commission.

Families At War

Our small villages made more than their fair share of sacrifices throughout the two World Wars. In many cases individual families were torn apart when father and sons went off to war, some never to return. Typical of those families were the Boyds of the Causey. The Causey lost nine men in the First World War and others made the supreme sacrifice in the Second World War. It is extraordinary that from such a small community three men received bravery awards, Frank Boyd D.S.C., Cecil Larmour M.M. and a young man from Coppy Lonnen named Hetherington who received the D.F.C. Colin Boyd of Bankwell House at the Causey is extremely proud of his family's contribution to the defence of our country and has provided the material for this feature. It is a privilege to relate the military story of this remarkable family.

Right: Robert Boyd (the head of the family) seated, served with the 10th Btn. Durham Light Infantry during the First World War. Joining the Army on 18th August 1914, prior to moving to the Causey, he was reputed to be the first man in Swalwell to volunteer for active service in the Great War. He was badly injured in the Battle of the Somme and because of incapacity invalided out on 27th July 1917. His health was so badly affected that he didn't enjoy a long life, he died in 1941 at the relatively young age of 54 years. Robert and his wife Amelia are featured on page 75. Four of their five sons served during the Second World War; William, Alan, Robert and Frank, Colin was too young.

Left: Robert Boyd jnr seen here on the left, served with the 1st Btn. D.L.I. during the Second World War. On the 23rd December 1941 and at the age of 23 years he lost his life. While on active service, the ship he was on went down off Tobruk on the North African coast. Sadly, along with everyone else on board, his remains were never recovered.

William Boyd, Royal Marines, Second World War. When the coal miners went on strike in 1926, William, aged 19 years, became a boxer to earn a living. A hardy character, he fought at Newcastle's St James Hall and at Edinburgh. He didn't hesitate to take on the old pros in the boxing booths on the Town Moor, or locally when they came to Swalwell or anywhere else. When the Second World War broke out he volunteered for service, stating that he wasn't a miner (a little white lie) which would have made him exempt. As a Marine he took part in the defence of the beleaguered island of Malta and in the invasion of Sicily.

Alan Boyd pictured at Darjeeling, India in 1933 while serving with the Black Watch. He was discharged in 1936 and returned to India to serve with the Calcutta Police from 1937 to 1947.

Frank Boyd, Merchant Navy. At the age of 22 years he was serving on board the SS *Temple Arch* sailing on a Russian Convoy during the Second World War. In April 1942 the ship was bombed and incapacitated by the German Luftwaffe, he and his subordinates were trapped in the engine room. They stayed at their posts and managed to restore engine power to enable the ship to manoeuvre out of danger. In recognition of his bravery and leadership he was awarded the Distinguished Service Cross. He was also presented with the 'Soviet Award' by the Government of the U.S.S.R.

The military service of the Boyd family continued when Mark, the grandson of Colin and Lillian Boyd, joined the Royal Military Police as a Regular Serviceman.

Robert Clark snr of Marley Hill during the First World War. He and his wife Hannah watched three sons go off to war, Matthew, George and Edward.

Edward Clark, Durham Light Infantry, the First World War. (Born 1898, died 1971.) He married Grace Brown of West Farm, Byermoor and they lived in Proudlocks Cottage. They had two children, Florence (pictured below) and Robert (featured on page 127) who lost his life in the Second World War.

Sergeant Matthew Clark (seated) killed in action, Battle of the Somme 1916. George Clark (standing) received severe facial injuries in the same battle, losing an eye. The little lad, Robert Clark, grew up to become the Manager of Laws (also Dales) at Burnopfield.

Florence Clark, pictured 22nd May 1942, served in the W.A.A.F. during the Second World War. Born 1st August 1919, she met and married George Wilson during the war, he too was a soldier. They had three children, Bob, Gary and Rita.

Leith Brown, Royal Navy, pictured in 1935. He was the brother of Grace Brown of West Farm, Byermoor, and served before and after the Second World War.

Thomas Crosson (centre rear) of Bowes Terrace, Andrews House. He served with the Northumberland Fusiliers in the First World War.

Jimmy Boyd of Sunniside, who served during the Second World War. He enlisted in the Royal Artillery but whilst on a visit to Scotland he was very impressed with the uniform of the Seaforth Highlanders. He was given the opportunity to try it on and as is evident the uniform is very eye catching.

Ernie Boyd (brother of Jimmy pictured left) served with the R.E.M.E. during the Second World War.

Margaret Rutherford (A.T.S.) of Streetgate, with her brother George (Northumberland Fusiliers) during the Second World War. Margaret married Bill Hudspith of Sunniside.

Sergeant Jack Rutherford, R.A.O.C., in the Middle East, 26th June 1941. (Brother of Margaret and George pictured left.)

John Laybourne, R.A.F., of Prospect Terrace, Sunniside served during the Second World War.

Robert Laybourne (brother of John), Yorkshire Light Infantry. He also served during the Second World War. The two brothers were cousins of Bill Hudspith.

Robert Douglas of Lingey Fine (eldest son of Stan) tragically drowned in an accident, *circa* 1942.

Michael Joyce of Byermoor. He and his wife Mary had four children, Michael, Margaret, Angela and Elizabeth.

Ronnie Warnaby of Byermoor during the Second World War. He was born on 3rd December 1926 and died 8th July 1978.

Joe Handy of Gibside Crescent, Byermoor. He served in the R.A.F during the Second World War.

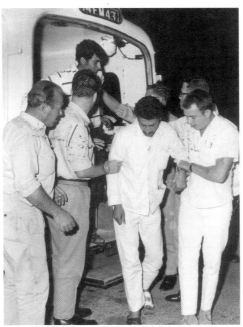

Byermoor-born Robert Andrew Graham, on the right, served in the Royal Army Medical Corp and is pictured here in Cyprus on duty as a Medical Orderly at the Military Hospital.

Ronnie Musgrove of the Hobson. In 1952 he joined the 11th Hussars shortly before his 18th birthday. He was selected to join the elite S.A.S. in 1953 and served with them until 1956. While based at Kuala Lumpur in Malaysia, he was on active service fighting Chinese Communists. After his military service he returned to work at the Hobson pit.

Terry Largue of Byermoor served with the Green Howards. He is pictured here on patrol in Northern Ireland in 1972. He survived a bullet wound during his service there, but having left the Army he tragically lost his life in the Piper Alpha oil rig explosion when 167 men died on 6th July 1988.

Paul Largue (brother of Terry) served in the Royal Regiment of Fusiliers. He is pictured here at Cambridge in 1978.

Lest We Forget

John Young of Byermoor (husband of Margaret Anne on page 99). Killed in action in the First World War.

Tribute to the R.A.F.
By
Winston Churchill

The gratitude of every home in our island, in our Empire, and indeed throughout the world, except in the abodes of the guilty, goes out to the British airmen who, undaunted by odds, unwearied in their constant challenge and mortal danger, are turning the tide of world war by their prowess and by their devotion.

Never in the field of human conflict was so much owed by so many to so few.

The Soldier
By
Rupert Brooke

If I should die, think only this of me,

That there's some corner of a foreign field that is forever England.

Robert Clark of Streetgate, pictured at Mount Clemence, Canada in 1943. In 1944 he lost his life over Germany when his Lancaster bomber was shot down. He and the rest of the crew were never returned to England.

Acknowledgements

There are many people deserving of our gratitude, especially those members of our History Society and members of the community at large who have produced so many wonderful photographs. We are greatly indebted to everyone of them, without their help this book could never have materialised. We would, however, wish to pay particular tribute to the following:

Our Society President, Mr Eddie Hayden of Marley Hill who has generated so many photographs and general information over the years, his contribution has been immeasurable.

Mary Brown for providing the cover photograph of Robbie Proudlock as a young lad. Society Secretary, Eleanor Baty for providing the back cover photograph of Marley Hill Miners.

Adele Evitt of Marley Hill School, Wendy and Eddie Liddle, Florence Wilson, Joan Hudson, Lena Brown, Edith and Jim Reid, Colin and Lillian Boyd, Ronnie Callaghan, Margaret Hudspith, Ernie and Joyce Boyd, David and Nancy Armstrong, Malcolm Taskas, Joe and Pauline Tate, Bob Lowdon, Rev. Alan Gales and Myra, Elsie and Gordon Harley, Linda and Frank Spraggon, Anne Henderson, Helen Douglas, Colin Scott, Eunice Turnbull, Robert Sowerby and Sheila Marley.

Colin Douglas for his well written articles and accompanying photographs.

Peter Davison who has provided so much valuable material.

John Caffrey for his computer expertise and his help when things go wrong. Margaret Newman for entering data and for proof reading. Andrew Clark of The People's History for his assistance and his advice throughout.

Sunniside Club Officials, Club Steward Alan Gowland and The Northern Clubs Federation Brewery for their continued and valued support.

The poem featured on page 119 can be found in *The Faber Book of War Poetry*.

We Dedicate This Book
To Members Of
The Sunniside & District Local History Society
Who Are Sadly No Longer With Us

The People's History

To find out more about this unique series of local history books – and to receive a catalogue of the latest titles – send a large stamped addressed envelope to:

The People's History
Suite 1
Byron House
Seaham Grange Business Park
Seaham
County Durham
SR7 0PW